Twayne's United States Authors Series

Sylvia E. Bowman, *Editor*

INDIANA UNIVERSITY

J. D. Salinger

TUSAS 40

(Revised Edition)

J. D. SALINGER

By WARREN FRENCH

REVISED EDITION

TWAYNE PUBLISHERS
A DIVISION OF G. K. HALL & CO., BOSTON

J. D. Salinger, Revised Edition

Warren French

First edition copyright © 1963 by Twayne Publishers, Inc.
Revised edition copyright © 1976 by G. K. Hall & Co.
All Rights Reserved

Published in 1976 by Twayne Publishers
A Division of G. K. Hall & Co.
70 Lincoln Street
Boston, Massachusetts 02111

Manufactured in the United States of America

Library of Congress Cataloging in Publication Data

French, Warren G. 1922–
J. D. Salinger.

(Twayne's United States authors series; 40)
Bibliography: p. 157–58
Includes index.
1. Salinger, Jerome David, 1919–
PS3537.A426Z6   1976   813'.5'4   76–910
ISBN 0–8057–7163–8
ISBN 0–8057–7447–5 (pbk.)

for
HANS ULHERR
(Coburg, Germany)
and

BOB GRIFFIN
(Berkeley, California)
who answered
when called upon

Contents

About the Author

Respectful of Salinger's desire for privacy, Warren French, the author of this first book-length study of the fiction-writer's work, has never met him and knows nothing of his private life; but he now also lives most of the year in the same rural New Hampshire town of Cornish—about twenty miles from Dartmouth College—that Salinger does.

Besides this book, Warren French has written articles about controversial points in Salinger's work and has edited a collection of essays about the American literature of the 1950s, viewing the decade as "The Age of Salinger." As a member of the editorial board of the new magazine *Creativity, Consciousness, and Human Ecology,* Professor French with Hume Mirza is now editing a symposium devoted to Salinger's relationship to Asiatic mystical thought.

Warren French also continues to teach American literature and film at Indiana University during the winter. He has also taught since World War II at colleges in Mississippi, Kentucky, Florida, Kansas, and Missouri; and he has visited many others.

Besides *J. D. Salinger,* he has contributed to the Twayne United States Authors Series books about John Steinbeck and Frank Norris; and he is completing a study of Joyce Cary. Besides the book of essays about the 1950s, he has edited similar collections of articles about the 1920s, the 1930s, and the 1940s. His interest in Steinbeck has also led to his writing *A Companion to "The Grapes of Wrath," A Filmguide to "The Grapes of Wrath,"* and *The Social Novel at the End of an Era,* a study of Steinbeck, William Faulkner, Ernest Hemingway, and Richard Wright. He has also edited, with Walter Kidd, *American Winners of the Nobel Prize in Literature.*

A native of Philadelphia and a graduate of the University of Pennsylvania, Warren French received his Doctor of Philosophy degree from the University of Texas. His principal interests besides writing are film collecting and historic preservation. He has made with H. Wayne Schuth several films—including

"Three New Orleans,' about legends of the Crescent City; and his major project is editing a series of critical books about important film-makers for the Twayne World Leaders Series. His permanent address is Cornish Flat, New Hampshire 03746.

Preface

When the original edition of this book about J. D. Salinger appeared in 1963, I think no one could have foretold that that year marked the climax of the productivity of what George Steiner has called the "Salinger Industry." I raced to complete my study before scholarly competitors published theirs, for I had read announcements that at least a dozen other studies were being prepared. None of these has appeared within the twelve years that have passed, and this book remains the only study of much more than fifty pages that examines from a single viewpoint Salinger's major work. However, five sizeable collections of essays, and an issue of *Wisconsin Studies in Contemporary Literature* devoted to Salinger, did appear during 1962 and 1963.

Since then the only substantial contributions to the study of Salinger have been made by James E. Miller, Jr., and by Kenneth Hamilton in pamphlets for a distinguished series about American and contemporary writers and also by a special issue of *Modern Fiction Studies*. Although at least four doctoral dissertations have been devoted to Salinger, as well as parts of many other theses and books about modern fiction, the number of articles published about him has fallen from a peak of thirty in 1963 to a consistent six in each year since 1970. Salinger himself has published since the appearance of my book in 1963 only *one* new story, "Hapworth 16, 1924" (*New Yorker*, June 19, 1965); and he has granted at most only two interviews.

This second edition of my book about Salinger appears at a time when his reputation is vastly different from what it was in 1963 when he was indeed—as Frederick L. Gwynn and Joseph L. Blotner described him in the first short book about him, *The Fiction of J. D. Salinger* (1958)—the author of "the only Post-War fiction unanimously approved by contemporary literate American youth." The purpose of my first edition, as announced in its preface, was to serve parents and teachers especially as "a guide for those who, bedeviled by the inscrutability of the younger generation, are not content simply to throw up their hands in despair but wish to understand."

This second edition is for a quite different audience. Although, when I inspect public and school libraries, I still find most books by and about Salinger being read, I also find that many young readers do not even recognize his name. There are, however, evidences—like Robert Cole's "Reconsideration" (*New Republic*, April 28, 1973)—that former readers, alienated from Salinger during the activist 1960s, are now returning to his books with renewed interest and are commending them to their children and their students. Rather than introducing an older generation to what a younger one is reading, as I hoped to do in 1963, this second edition may now introduce a younger generation to what their parents of the "silent generation" of the 1950s read with enthusiasm because they thought Salinger voiced their views of the "phony" world.

I do not mean to imply that the time has come to relegate Salinger to the museum in which Holden Caulfield of *The Catcher in the Rye* finds what solace his world offers. I think that many readers are like Ernest W. Ranly (*Commonweal*, February 23, 1973) who, upon reading *Franny and Zooey*, found it "weird and disappointing"; but he—and perhaps others—are now returning to find the book "an extremely warm and rewarding experience." Since the activist fervor of the 1960s has subsided and since the Eastern philosophies and meditation movements that attracted Salinger years ago and that led him to flee from his fame at its height are now beginning to be more widely understood, today's readers are turning to his books not for his scathing condemnation of the "phony" society that he and his contemporaries hated but for his embodiment in fiction of principles of the contemplative life that they seek to enter.

Because of these changed conditions, I was tempted to rewrite this book to suit the interests of a new audience; but I have overcome this temptation. Except for the correction of small errors, the body of the text is untouched. As I explained in my original preface, strongly influenced by the argument in Wayne C. Booth's then new *The Rhetoric of Fiction* (1961), "we regard a 'successful' story as one in which there is a rhetorical justification for everything included." As a result, I sought in the text of my book "to concentrate upon analyzing the effects achieved through the rhetorical techniques employed." Even then I observed—with a seeming prescience I cannot claim—that this "first structural analysis of the whole body of Salinger's work before 1960" came at a time that "a phase of his career" was ended and that "a self-contained study" might, therefore, be made of it. However, the value to this account of how Salinger's work appeared to one analytical enthusiast at this climactic point in his career deters me from tampering with it; for, as has been noted, Salinger's new phase has not developed. I have elsewhere in a discussion of "The Age of Salinger" (*The Fifties: Fiction, Poetry, Drama*, 1971) explained the way in which we can see in retrospect how Salinger served as the outstanding literary spokesman for the pervasive defeatism of the 1950s.

I have completely revised and updated the bibliography accompanying this book. Since other scholars have been as frustrated as I have myself been about the omission from the first edition of details about the original publication of Salinger's short stories, I have included summary publication histories of all of his works. Since most essays written about him before 1962 have been reprinted in one or several collections, I have generally limited critical notes to the few more recent articles that I have found of value. Since Salinger's "Hapworth 16, 1924" had not appeared when this book was first published, I stress references to interpretations of it. I did not add my own since to me the story contributes little to the social criticism in Salinger's work upon which I had concentrated.

I have been disappointed to find that few recent critics of Salinger have gone beyond the analysis of this social criticism, especially since Salinger's "alienation" from the world has received what seems to be definitive analyses in James E. Miller, Jr.'s *J. D. Salinger* (1965), which includes a valuable interpretation of "Hapworth 16, 1924," and in Clinton W. Trowbridge's "The Symbolic Structure of *The Catcher in the Rye*" (*Sewanee Review*, Summer 1966). Even the sensitive positive readings by James Bryan—one of the most prolific recent critics—of some of Salinger's most controversial works seem to be limited by their attention to subjects that no longer attract readers to Salinger's work.

A "new" criticism of Salinger is needed and has been developing, though slowly. The first "new" stirring—one which came in the very year that Professor Trowbridge and *Modern Fiction Studies* capped the "old" criticism—was a disparaging attack on Salinger's fiction by Richard W. Noland in "The Novel of Personal Formula: J. D. Salinger" (*University Review*, Autumn 1966). Noland argues correctly that the members of the Glass family "have little or no interest in society; they are concerned about their own salvation." This insight causes Noland to ask, however, how Salinger "can produce great fiction when he is not really interested in the social and moral complexities of everyday life, or in that perennial subject of fiction—the relation of the individual to society?"

This inescapable question has not yet been adequately answered; but the constructive beginning of a "new" criticism of Salinger came—quite appropriately—with a new decade in Helen Weinberg's *The New Novel in America: The Kafkan Mode in Contemporary Fiction* (1970) which dispenses with psychological criticism of Salinger and which argues cogently that "It is not necessary for him to rebel against the secular as it is found in the community . . . , for he does not recognize the community. He sees only individuals, and he sees only one group, the family group." Weinberg's work is, however, only a start in a new direction because, rigidly limited by a Kafkan model, she concludes that Buddy Glass's "spiritual quest," like that of Kafka's "K" in *The Castle*, inevitably fails.

Different appreciations of Salinger need to be related not to social and conventional religious concerns but to transcendent philosophies. Although Bernice and Sanford Goldstein have shown the basic influences of Zen on Salinger's work, their group of useful essays constitutes only an elementary textbook. The reasons to read Salinger—as people like Robert Coles and Ernest Ranly are discovering—are as urgent today as they were a quarter century ago; for Salinger still presents a challenge to enlightened and enlightening criticism. This book will serve its purpose if it provides a guide to what has been done and if it helps inspire what needs to be done.

WARREN FRENCH

Cornish, New Hampshire

Acknowledgments

Chapter II, "The Phony and Nice Worlds," has appeared in the January, 1963, issue of *Wisconsin Studies in Contemporary Literature* and appears in this book slightly revised with the consent of the editors. I also wish to thank Harper and Row, Publishers, for permission to use brief quotations from *Salinger: A Critical and Personal Portrait,* edited and introduced by Henry Anatole Grunwald (© 1962 by Henry Anatole Grunwald), an anthology which makes conveniently accessible much previous Salinger criticism. I especially wish to thank Donald Fiene, of Louisville, Kentucky, for kindly making available to me many results of his extensive research, which is to be incorporated into his own forthcoming biographical and bibliographical study, *J. D. Salinger in the Twentieth Century.*

If this book reflects at all the views of contemporary youth it is because Marc Rosenberg, an undergraduate English major at the University of Pennsylvania, first insisted that it be written and then read the manuscript with a critical eye. My debt to my two other principal abettors is, I hope, partly repaid by the dedication. I am also grateful to Sylvia Bowman, for allowing me the pleasure of writing about Salinger, and to Mrs. Madge Tams of the University of Florida Library for her encouragement and resourcefulness in locating materials.

Chronology

1919   Jerome David Salinger born January 1 in New York City, second child and only son of Sol and Miriam Jillich Salinger.
1932   Enrolled in McBurney School, Manhattan.
1934   Enrolled in Valley Forge Military Academy, Pennsylvania.
1935   Literary editor of *Crossed Sabres*, Valley Forge Military Academy yearbook.
1936   Graduates from Valley Forge Military Academy in June.
1937–   Attends summer session at New York University; visits
1938   Europe and lives briefly in Vienna and Poland; briefly attends Ursinus College, Collegetown, Pennsylvania.
1939   Attends Whit Burnett's short-story writing class at Columbia University.
1940   First short story, "The Young Folks," published in Whit Burnett's *Story* magazine; "Go See Eddie" in *University of Kansas City Review*.
1941   "The Hang of It" in *Collier's*; "The Heart of a Broken Story" in *Esquire*. Sells first story about Holden Caulfield to *New Yorker* (revised version not published until 1946). Classified 1-B by Selective Service. Works as entertainer on *M. S. Kungsholm*.
1942   "The Long Debut of Lois Taggett" in *Story*; "Personal Notes of an Infantryman" in *Collier's*. Reclassified and drafted into United States Army; attends Officers, First Sergeants, and Instructors School of the Signal Corps.
1943   Stationed in Nashville, Tennessee, with rank of Staff Sergeant; applies for Officers' Candidate School; transferred to Army Counter-Intelligence Corps. "The Varioni Brothers," his first short story to be published in *Saturday Evening Post*.
1944   Counter-Intelligence training at Tiverton, Devonshire, England; assigned to Fourth Division, United States Army; lands on Utah Beach, Normandie, on D-Day, June 6; participates in five campaigns in Europe as

Security Agent for Twelfth Infantry Regiment. "Both Parties Concerned," "Soft-Boiled Sergeant," "Last Day of the Last Furlough" in *Saturday Evening Post*; "Once a Week Won't Kill You" in *Story*.

1945 Discharged from army. "Elaine" in *Story*; "A Boy in France" in *Saturday Evening Post*; "This Sandwich Has No Mayonnaise" in *Esquire*; "The Stranger" and "I'm Crazy" (first story to use material incorporated into *The Catcher in the Rye*) in *Collier's*.

1946 Ninety-page novelette about Holden Caulfield accepted for publication but withdrawn by Salinger who makes belated *New Yorker* debut with "Slight Rebellion Off Madison," another forerunner of *The Catcher in the Rye*.

1947 "A Young Girl in 1941 with No Waist at All" in *Mademoiselle*; "The Inverted Forest," major uncollected work, in *Cosmopolitan*.

1948 Begins long, exclusive association with *New Yorker* with "A Perfect Day for Bananafish" (January 31); "Uncle Wiggily in Connecticut" and "Just Before the War with the Eskimos" also in *New Yorker*; older "A Girl I Knew" in *Good Housekeeping*, also selected for *Best American Short Stories of 1949*; "Blue Melody" in *Cosmopolitan*. Moves to Westport, Connecticut.

1949 "The Laughing Man" in *New Yorker*: "Down at the Dinghy" in *Harper's*.

1950 "For Esmé—with Love and Squalor" in *New Yorker* and *Prize Stories of 1950*. "My Foolish Heart," film version of "Uncle Wiggily in Connecticut," produced by Samuel Goldwyn; starred in by Susan Hayward and Dana Andrews; released on January 21.

1951 *The Catcher in the Rye* published July 16. Salinger visits Europe. "Pretty Mouth and Green My Eyes" in *New Yorker*.

1952 "De Daumier-Smith's Blue Period" in *World Review* (London), Salinger's only story to be first published abroad and his last one for a magazine other than the *New Yorker*. Salinger visits Mexico. Selected as one of three distinguished alumni of the year by the Valley Forge Military Academy.

1953 Moves to Cornish, New Hampshire. Meets Claire Douglas. "Teddy" in *New Yorker* (January 31). *Nine Stories* published April 6.

1955   Marries Claire Douglas on February 17. "Franny" and "Raise High the Roof Beam, Carpenters" in *New Yorker*. Daughter, Margaret Ann, born December 10.

1957   "Zooey" in *New Yorker* (May 4).

1959   "Seymour: An Introduction" in *New Yorker* (June 6).

1960   Son, Matthew, born February 13.

1961   *Franny and Zooey* published September 14.

1963   *"Raise High the Roof Beam, Carpenters"* and *"Seymour: An Introduction"* published January 28.

1965   "Hapworth 16, 1924" in *New Yorker* (June 19).

1967   Divorce granted Claire at Newport, New Hampshire, in November.

1974   *Complete Uncollected Short Stories of J. D. Salinger,* an unauthorized edition published, apparently in Berkeley, California; denounced by Salinger in his first public statement in years—a telephone call to Lacey Fosburgh—reported in *New York Times,* November 3.

CHAPTER *1*

"That David Copperfield Kind of Crap"

Success is counted sweetest
By those who ne'er succeed

EMILY DICKINSON

JEROME DAVID SALINGER has been even less willing than his creation Holden Caulfield to share with an avidly curious public "that David Copperfield kind of crap" about "his lousy childhood . . . and all that." Despite what might be termed Salinger's "reverse exhibitionism," enough is known about his literary career and enough more has leaked out about his personal life to enable us to see that his story is the not unusual one of the lad who courted fame until, upon having the rare luck of winning her hand, he discovered that she brought with her a retinue of nuisances.

I *Pursuit*

Salinger's birth date is always given as January 1, 1919—although it seems curious that a man reluctant to divulge information about himself was born on such a seemingly arbitrary day as New Year's. His parents are as shadowy figures as Holden Caulfield's in *The Catcher in the Rye*. His father, Sol Salinger, was born in Cleveland, Ohio, and is said to have been the son of a rabbi;[1] but he drifted sufficiently far from orthodox Judaism to become an importer of hams and to marry a gentile, Scotch-Irish Marie Jillich, who changed her name to Miriam to fit better into her husband's family. Salinger has one living sibling, a sister Doris, who is eight years older than he and who is a dress buyer at Bloomingdale's department store.[2]

Salinger's childhood has never been publicly discussed. He attended schools on Manhattan's upper west side, where he apparently did satisfactory work, except in arithmetic. Like many sons of upper-middle-class New York families, he probably spent many summers in upstate or New England camps. During the summer of 1930, when he was eleven, he was voted "the most popular actor" at Camp Wigwam, Harrison, Maine.[3] At the time he should have begun high school in 1932, he was transferred to a private institution, Manhattan's famed McBurney School, where he told the interviewer that he was interested in dramatics; but he reportedly flunked out after a year.[4] In September, 1934, his father enrolled him at Valley Forge Military Academy in Pennsylvania.

Salinger spent two years at Valley Forge, graduating in June, 1936. His career there, based on materials in his "201 file," has been thoroughly discussed by Frederick Pillsbury in the Philadelphia *Bulletin*.[5] Salinger was surely no Holden Caulfield in the classroom; his grades were satisfactory but not distinguished. His marks in English varied from 75 to 92. His final grades were: English, 88; French, 88; German, 76; History, 79; Dramatics, 88. As recorded in his Valley Forge file, his I.Q. was 115. While such scores must be treated with caution, this one and another of 111 that he made when tested in New York[6] are strong evidence that he was slightly above the average in intelligence, but far from the "genius" or even "superior" category. There is no evidence, incidentally, that like the prodigious Glasses he ever participated in a children's quiz show; but from the way he writes about such programs, he probably thought that he should have.

Salinger—no recluse at Valley Forge—belonged to the Glee Club, the Aviation Club, the French Club, the Non-Commissioned Officers' Club, and Mask and Spur (a dramatic organization); and he also served during his senior year as literary editor of *Crossed Sabres,* the academy yearbook. While it cannot be determined how much he may have contributed anonymously to this book, he signed a three-stanza poetic tribute to the academy that has since been set to music and is still sung by the cadets at their last formation before graduation.[7] He might also have written the class prophecy predicting that he would write "four-act melodramas for the Boston Philharmonic Orchestra." While at Valley Forge, Salinger began writing short stories, working by flashlight under his blankets after official "lights out." He also appeared to be intensely interested in getting into the movies or in selling some of his work to Hollywood.

The six years after his graduation from Valley Forge are among the least accurately documented of his adult life. The most detailed source of information about them is the interview that he granted Shirley Blaney, a high school correspondent for the Claremont, New Hampshire, *Daily Eagle*. There seems no reason to question the interview's general accuracy, even though it appears unlikely that Salinger attended New York University for two years, as Miss Blaney states. What he did immediately after graduating from Valley Forge is unknown; but he was enrolled at the Washington Square College of New York University at least for the 1937 summer session. He has several times stated that when he was eighteen and nineteen he spent some time in Vienna and Poland (possibly in Bydgoszcz)—either with or without his father[8]—while learning German and the details of the ham importing business. Since it is unlikely that he would have remained in Austria after Hitler's *Anschluss,* March 12-13, 1938, he probably went to Europe in the fall of 1937 and returned home as the political situation abroad became critical.

In the autumn of 1938, Salinger enrolled at Ursinus College, a coeducational institution sponsored by the Evangelical and Reformed Church at Collegeville, Pennsylvania, not far from Valley Forge. For nine weeks, he wrote a humorous and critical column, "The Skipped Diploma," for the *Ursinus Weekly,* but he told Miss Blaney that lack of interest caused him to quit school at mid-year and return to New York to enroll in Whit Burnett's famous course in short-story writing at Columbia University.[9] According to Ernest Havemann, Burnett was not at first impressed with the quiet boy, who made no comments and was interested primarily in playwrighting; but Salinger's first story, "The Young Folks," which he turned in near the end of the semester, was polished enough to use in *Story,* edited by Burnett.[10]

After first breaking into print in March, 1940, in this magazine that is famous for discovering new, young talent,[11] Salinger enjoyed no further successes for a year. Then in 1941—when he was only twenty-two—he hit the well-paying mass circulation magazines with a "short, short story" in *Collier's* and with a "satire" in *Esquire*. He even almost made the *New Yorker*. This magazine, with which he was eventually to become exclusively associated, purchased "Slight Rebellion Off Madison," the first story to mention Holden Caulfield; but it decided not to publish this story of a mixed-up kid when our entry into World War II meant that most such young American men were headed for military service.[12]

Salinger also told Shirley Blaney that during 1941 he had worked as an entertainer on the Swedish liner *M. S. Kungsholm*. This statement would seem to be verified by Salinger's reference, in a 1947 story "A Young Girl in 1941 with No Waist At All," to the *Kungsholm's* visit to Havana during its last cruise before being seized by the United States government for use as a troopship; this reference seems hardly coincidental and does correspond with the facts. If Salinger was on the *Kungsholm* during its last Caribbean cruise, he spent the day of the Pearl Harbor attack at sea, since the ship did not dock in New York until Monday, December 8, 1941.

Once the United States was at war, Salinger wrote Colonel Milton G. Baker,* adjutant at Valley Forge Military Academy, that he wished to enter the service, but had been classified 1-B due to a slight cardiac condition.[13] He asked what kind of defense work he might do; but it was not long before Selective Service standards were lowered enough so that he was drafted in 1942. Along with a second Salinger short story, Whit Burnett published in *Story* (September, 1942) a letter announcing that Salinger was attending the Officers, First Sergeants, and Instructors School of the Signal Corps. William Maxwell adds that during the first part of his military service Salinger corrected papers in a ground school for aviation cadets, probably in Nashville, Tennessee; from there, on June 2, 1943, Salinger again wrote to Colonel Baker to request support of his application for Officers' Candidate School.[14] Instead of going to OCS, by which he said he thought he had only a slight chance of being accepted, he was apparently transferred to the Air Service Command in Dayton, Ohio, where Maxwell reports he wrote publicity releases. At the end of 1943, Salinger was transferred

---

* Lt. General Baker is now Superintendent of Valley Forge Military Academy and President of the Reserve Officers Association.

again to the Counter-Intelligence Corps.[15] He was also corresponding in 1943 with Eugene O'Neill's daughter Oona (now Mrs. Charlie Chaplin) in Hollywood.

In the meantime, he continued to write whenever he found the opportunity. *Collier's* had used another "short, short story" in its issue of December 12, 1942; and Tom Davis reports that during the same year *Stag*, a man's magazine, purchased the short story "Paula," which has never been published.[16] In 1943, Salinger broke into the well-paying and celebrated *Saturday Evening Post* with "The Varioni Brothers," a story of wasted genius in the corrupt 1920's. In the same letter in which he asked Colonel Baker to support his application for OCS, Salinger confided that his agent hoped that the *Post* story might be bought by Hollywood. The movie-makers disappointed Salinger, but he found a steady market for his stories. Three more appeared in the *Post* in 1944; in the last of these, "The Last Day of the Last Furlough," a character named Holden Caulfield is first mentioned in print. Near the end of the year, *Story* printed "Once a Week Won't Kill You," and Whit Burnett disclosed that Staff Sergeant Salinger had sent from overseas two hundred dollars of his earnings from the "slicks" to be used to encourage other writers and to be applied if possible to prizes for the magazine's annual contest for college undergraduates (which Norman Mailer had won in 1941.)

By this time Salinger was in the thick of the war. After training in Tiverton, Devonshire (an English town much like that in "For Esmé—with Love and Squalor"), he had joined the American Army's Fourth Division and landed on Utah Beach five hours after the initial assault wave on D-Day. He then moved with the Division through five European campaigns, serving as a special agent responsible for the security of the Twelfth Infantry Regiment.[18] A tale also circulates that he met Ernest Hemingway when the author-correspondent visited Salinger's regiment, and that Salinger became disgusted when Hemingway shot the head off a chicken to demonstrate the merits of a German Luger. (Certainly Salinger since the war has constantly sniped at Hemingway, although he has avoided unfavorable references to other living writers.) Undocumented reports also circulate that sometime during the war he married a Frenchwoman who was a doctor—possibly a psychiatrist.[19] Salinger has never admitted this marriage and the records of the Florida

Bureau of Vital Statistics fail to indicate that a divorce was granted in that state in 1947 to Jerome David Salinger, as Ernest Havemann asserts it was.[20]

Despite his military duties of interrogating civilians and captured soldiers in an effort to locate Gestapo agents, Salinger found time to continue his writing. More of his stories were published in 1945 than in any other year except 1948. He made his last contributions to the *Saturday Evening Post* and to *Story* during this year, and he began to contribute once more to the first two "slicks" in which he had published—*Esquire* and *Collier's*. One of his contributions to *Collier's*, "I'm Crazy," which appeared in the Christmas issue, marked the long delayed literary debut of Holden Caulfield, who had been mentioned as missing in action in several wartime stories. Holden appeared again in 1946 when the appearance of the long deferred "Slight Rebellion Off Madison" was the occasion of Salinger's debut in the *New Yorker*.

William Maxwell reports that a publisher was ready to publish an earlier version of *Catcher*, a ninety-page novelette, but that Salinger was dissatisfied and decided to do the book over.[21] Meanwhile Salinger, out of the army, tried to support himself by writing for the "slicks." The May, 1947, issue of *Mademoiselle* carried "A Young Girl in 1941 with No Waist at All," a nostalgic attempt to recapture American youth's prewar innocence; and the December *Cosmopolitan* featured as its "novelette complete in one issue," "The Inverted Forest," Salinger's longest work prior to *The Catcher in the Rye* and an involved, obscure allegory of the artist, his possible muses, and his fate that Salinger has since attempted to keep from being reprinted.[22] During at least part of this period, Salinger was living on Park Avenue with his parents and squiring an assortment of girls to Greenwich Village at night. He had also begun to develop the enthusiasm for Zen Buddhism that has often been reflected in works like "Teddy" and "Seymour," even though there is no indication that Salinger really grasps the principles of this paradox-ridden Oriental cult.[23]

Salinger finally attained some measure of the recognition for which he had been struggling in 1948, when three of his stories— "A Perfect Day for Bananafish," "Uncle Wiggily in Connecticut," and "Just Before the War with the Eskimos"—appeared in the *New Yorker* and, according to Martha Foley,[24] won him a contract with this magazine that, despite its critics, is considered the top of the heap by most young people who aspire to be recognized as serious creative writers. Two stories also appeared outside the *New Yorker* in this busy year. *Good Housekeeping* printed "A Girl I Know," recollections of prewar Vienna that won Salinger, for the first time, a place in Miss Foley's *Best American Short Stories* of the year collection; and "Blue Melody," Salinger's version of the Bessie Smith legend, appeared in *Cosmopolitan.* He also sold an early story about the Glass family, "Ocean Full of Bowling Balls," to *Woman's Home Companion,* but the publisher refused to use the story in either that magazine or *Collier's* and eventually Salinger withdrew it.

After 1948, his pace of writing slackened. During 1949, "The Laughing Man" appeared in the *New Yorker* and "Down at the Dinghy" in *Harper's.* During 1950, he published only the memorable "For Esmé—with Love and Squalor" in the *New Yorker.* Presumably all through this period he was trying to make a novel out of his stories of Holden Caulfield. He probably found the task burdensome, because he once said that he thought of himself as "a dash man and not a miler" and thought it probable that he would never write a novel.[25]

He also came as close to mingling with his public during this period as at any time in his career. He moved from New York City to Tarrytown, New York—a famed Hudson River community where Washington Irving had resided—and from there to Westport, Connecticut, a fashionable exurbanite community, where he lived with a Schnauzer named Benny.[26] He even paid one visit to a short-story class at Sarah Lawrence College, after which William Maxwell reports that Salinger said, "I enjoyed the day, but it isn't something I'd ever want to do again."[27] Disturbed with himself for becoming "oracular" and "labelling" all the writers he respected, he has since avoided all such "public performances," although his name alone would surely guarantee the success of any writers' conference or summer literary workshop.

He also had, on January 21, 1950, the experience at long last of seeing the motion picture version of one of his works released. The Samuel Goldwyn studios had converted "Uncle Wiggily in Connecticut" into "My Foolish Heart," an "adult" romance starring popular Susan Hayward and Dana Andrews. The *New Yorker,* and presumably Salinger himself, vigorously disapproved of what Hollywood had made of the story; and, despite his early yearnings to break into the movies, Salinger has since consistently refused to sell screen or television rights to any of his other works. The script of "My Foolish Heart" has never been printed, but one of the most curious pieces of Salingeriana is a 128-page pamphlet entitled *Mit Dumme Hjerte,* which contains a story in Danish that Victor Skaarup built around the motion picture.

Although his experiences at Sarah Lawrence and with Samuel Goldwyn had probably already made Salinger suspect that success could be embarrassing, what William James calls the "bitch-goddess" caught up with him with a vengeance in 1951 after the publication on July 16 of *The Catcher in the Rye,* product of ten years' labor. But *Catcher* was not actually the immediate enormous success that Salinger's adoration squad fancies in retrospect. It had an uphill struggle for two years before establishing itself at the top of the junk-sculpture heap of postwar fiction. Salinger did allow it to be made the midsummer selection of the Book-of-the-Month Club and even permitted fellow novelist William Maxwell to quote him in a biographical sketch in the club's magazine (Salinger rejected all book club offers for *Franny and Zooey*); but Charles Lee in his history of the club reports that *Catcher* was "not especially liked by the membership."[28]

The first reviewers far from agreed on the merits of the book. Only the *New Yorker* (August 11, 1951), to which Salinger contributed, rolled out the red carpet with a five-page laudation by another contributor, playwright S. N. Behrman. The *New York Times* and *Herald Tribune* were evasive; Virgilia Peterson dodged the issue in the *Herald Tribune* (July 15, 1951) with the statement that the opinion of Holden Caulfield's contemporaries would "constitute the real test of Mr. Salinger's validity." The specifically literary journals—*Booklist, Library Journal, Saturday Review*—were impressed; but except for *Harper's Monthly,* the more thoughtful general magazines—*New Republic, Nation, Atlantic*—were less so. The *United States Quarterly Book Review* (sponsored by the Library of Congress) and the *Catholic World* launched the long procession of complaints against the excessive use of teen-age profanity. The dissident viewpoint was summed up in *Commentary,* a publication of the American Jewish Committee, by William Poster, an editor of the *American Mercury,*

who attacked both the novel and the *"New Yorker* school."
Catcher, he said, could be distinguished from comic strips like
"Our Bill" and "Penny"—with which it had much in common—
not "by superior depth but a different kind of selectivity and a
different set of conventions." The *New Yorker* "school," he
asserted, "has run down because it cannot be recharged from the
battery of some viable, positive approach to culture, morals,
religion, or politics."[29]

   Catcher did not at first sell as well as *Franny and Zooey*
has. Although it made the "best-seller" list in the *New York
Times,* it never reached the top. *The Caine Mutiny, From Here
to Eternity,* and Nicholas Monsarrat's *The Cruel Sea* monopolized
the first three positions during the ten weeks from August 19
to October 21, 1951 when *Catcher* reached fourth place—the
peak of its popularity. It remained on the list only twenty-nine
weeks, about as long as *Franny and Zooey* was in first place.
It last appeared in twelfth place on March 2, 1952, while
Herman Wouk's nautical fantasy remained on top and monopolized the year's awards for the best novel.

   The novel was successful enough, however, to upset Salinger.
He was disturbed first by the enormous photograph of his face
on the dust-jacket. At his request, it was removed from the third
and subsequent impressions of the book. He was less successful
in avoiding interview, advice, and autograph-hunters. Although
he admitted to Eloise Perry Hazard that "many of the letters
from readers have been very nice," he told her "I feel tremendously relieved that the season for success for *The Catcher in
the Rye* is nearly over. I enjoyed a small part of it, but most
of it I found hectic and professionally and personally demoraliz-
ing."[30] Miss Perry reported that to avoid publicity Salinger had
bolted for Europe.

   He returned to find that the "season for success" had not died
down. Valley Forge Military Academy selected him in 1952 as
one of its three distinguished alumni of the year and asked him
to attend a ceremony to receive an award. His sister Doris
replied that he was in Mexico and could not attend. On June
25, however, he wrote personally to thank the academy for the
handsome award, which he said made him somewhat uneasy.[31]
With the publication, in March, 1953, of the paperback edition
that has since sold over 1,250,000 copies,[32] Salinger began to
"enjoy" his reputation as—to cite poet Stanley Kunitz—"the only

young novelist . . . praised vociferously" by English majors and writing students.[33]

II *Flight*

When the excitement over *Catcher* did not die down, Salinger left Westport for Cornish, New Hampshire, where he has since resided in a house on a dirt road some distance from town. Not long after he moved there, his second book, *Nine Stories,* collecting all that he wished to preserve of his early short stories, appeared in April, 1953. Although *Nine Stories* never rose above ninth place on the *New York Times* "best-seller" list, it had the distinction—unique for a book of short stories—of remaining on the list for over three months. It has remained steadily in print since 1954 in a paperbound edition, and the stories have been translated at least into Danish and German.

During his first year in Cornish, Salinger visited the nearby Dartmouth College library, participated in social functions (he met his future wife, Claire Douglas, at a cocktail party in Manchester, New Hampshire),[34] and palled around with high school students, attending their basketball games and entertaining them at record parties. In November, 1953, he even granted Shirley Blaney the interview for the high school page of the Claremont, New Hampshire, *Daily Eagle.* He reputedly became annoyed, however, when this interview did not appear on the high school page as scheduled but was featured on the editorial page several days later on November 13. He ceased entertaining the high schoolers, and later, when they visited his house, they found a high fence around it.[35]

At the time Salinger may have been disturbed that the girl he would later marry had entered into a brief marriage with a Harvard business school student; he may also have been annoyed by an increasing number of curiosity seekers. When the interview he granted Shirley Blaney was given more prominence than he had anticipated, he may have supposed that he was being exploited by the last members of the public he trusted and that, therefore, he must withdraw altogether into a circle of intimate friends whom he could importune not to talk about him. Whatever the reasons, the year of 1954 is a blank in his history.

He broke his long silence in January, 1955, with the publication in the *New Yorker* of "Franny," the first of the stories about the

Glass family which have occupied him for nearly a decade. Jack Skow describes this story, which has been enormously popular with college people, as Salinger's wedding gift to Claire Douglas, the London-born Radcliffe girl whom he surprised the world by marrying at Barnard, Vermont, on February 17, 1955.[36] On December 10 of the same year, the Salingers became the parents of a daughter, Margaret Ann. Since then Salinger has devoted himself principally to two families: his own and the Glasses. His own was augmented on February 13, 1960, when his son Matthew was born; the Glass legend was developed with the publication in November, 1955, of "Raise High the Roofbeam, Carpenters," the story of Seymour Glass's wedding day; in May, 1957, of "Zooey," a continuation of "Franny"; and finally in June, 1959, of "Seymour: An Introduction," a garrulous character sketch of a Central Park West seer in which Salinger deliberately confuses his own personality with that of his narrator, so that—as Eliot Fremont-Smith points out—it is no longer possible to tell "who's who, and who is real."[37]

Few people have seen Salinger during the last decade; but his reputation and the excitement about his work continue to grow. His fiction has been translated into Italian, French, German, Dutch, Swedish, Norwegian, Danish, Japanese, Hebrew, Serbo-Croatian, Czech, Finnish, and other languages. It has even become popular in Russia, where possession of a copy of *The Catcher in the Rye* has become a status symbol among discontented adolescents.[38] A poll conducted among American literature instructors in Southern California by Henry Dan Piper placed both Salinger and *The Catcher in the Rye* at the head of the lists of those authors and books published since 1941 that have achieved the stature of modern classics.[39] Even William Faulkner hailed *The Catcher in the Rye* as the "best" work of "the present generation of writing," because it "expresses so completely" what Faulkner himself tried to say and because Holden exemplifies the tragedy of youth in that, "when he attempted to enter the human race, there was no human race there."[40]

Excitement over Salinger reached what may prove to be its apogee in September, 1961, when the already much-discussed "Franny" and "Zooey" were published in a book with a few witty and misleading remarks by Salinger on the dust-jacket in lieu of an announced thousand-word introduction. The book almost immediately shot into first place on the *New York Times Book Review*'s list of best-sellers and remained there for six months. Even though Salinger refused to permit book clubs to circulate the work, it sold more than 125,000 copies within two weeks after its publication. Prominent writers and critics like John Updike and Alfred Kazin were called upon to write long review essays of the work. The publishers fought vainly against the twin scourges of today's book trade—those who place books on sale before the publication date and the discount houses.[41] Advertisements needed to consist of nothing but the name of the book and its author. It was the book-seller's dream come true— a work that literally sells itself.

Through all this excitement, Salinger's own voice could be heard only in connection with the arrangements for the publication of a British edition. Dissatisfied with his previous publisher, who had allowed a volume of Salinger's short stories to be published in a paperback volume with a lurid cover, Salinger reportedly at first proposed that someone else do the book and turn the royalties over to his former publisher to be turned over in turn to the Authors' Society.[42] Finally he sold the rights to William Heinemann for an advance of four thousand pounds, although another publisher had offered ten thousand. Salinger also rejected the British Book Society's offer to take the work, just as he had those of American clubs.[43]

While translations of *Franny and Zooey* are doubtless being prepared, Salinger continues to lead a life much like that Holden Caulfield dreamed of when he said that he would pretend to be a deaf-mute and hide his children. Salinger's wife and two youngsters live behind a high fence in their Cornish home, while Salinger himself works principally in a nearby concrete bunker. This structure may have been inspired by the small castle at Muzot, where Rainer Maria Rilke, the German poet whom Salinger intensely admires, enjoyed in February, 1922, during his forty-seventh year, the great burst of inspiration that enabled him to complete the *Duino Elegies* and the *Sonnets to Orpheus*.

Despite Salinger's assertion on the dust-jacket of *Franny and Zooey* that he is busy, he has published little since his marriage. The publication in a single volume in 1963 of "Raise High the Roof Beam, Carpenters" and "Seymour: An Introduction" marks the collection of all of his most recent work, which is apparently all that he wishes collected. His seclusion may actually result from an inability to make the social adjustments expected of mature members of society. His reaction to his single experience in coping with inquisitive students at Sarah Lawrence and the repeated reports of his running away from people who attempt to speak to him suggest that he finds it as difficult as his character Raymond Ford in "The Inverted Forest" to relax around strangers. Although some critics have pointlessly chided Salinger for his inaccessibility, he should—if interviews embarrass him— be left alone. Those who hound him might well ponder William Faulkner's impassioned statement of his belief:

> . . . that only a writer's works were in the public domain, to be discussed and investigated and written about. . . . But that, until the writer committed a crime or ran for public office, his private life was his own; and not only had he the right to defend that privacy, but the public had the duty to do so since one man's liberty must stop at exactly the point where the next one's begins.[44]

Salinger's refusal to grant adaptation rights to his work is less defensible than his shunning publicity. Although we may sympathize with his desire to keep his work from being distorted as it was by those responsible for the film "My Foolish Heart," Salinger's reported comment, when Elia Kazan requested the right to dramatize *The Catcher in the Rye*, that "Holden wouldn't like it"[45] is either contemptuous facetiousness or the result of really startling intellectual immaturity. Whatever the reason for his distrust of responsible artists in the visual media that had once enchanted him, his ban on production of dramatic adaptations of his work has been so drastic that the only such production that I have heard of being publicly presented was Barbara Wells's dramatization of two scenes about Holden Caulfield, which were offered on June 7-9, 1962, at the Repertory Theatre Circle in New York.[46]

Salinger's refusal since 1954 to grant anthologists the right to reprint unaltered specimens of his work, and his efforts actually to prevent the publication of his previous work or criticisms of it, is not at all defensible, for, as Faulkner also observed in the statement quoted above, when a writer submits his work for publication and accepts money for it, he "must accept whatever the public wished to say about [it] from praise to burning." Yet Salinger even implied in a letter to Donald Fiene that if any interpretation of his work were needed, he would supply it himself. Such an attitude suggests a childishly petulant desire not to let anybody else play with his toys. If Salinger is really as intent as he claims upon his own new work, we may wonder why he bothers to overstep the point where "the next man's liberty begins."

Salinger has been remarkably successful in withholding information about his personal tastes from a public that covets such "inside dope," although the nervous strain of preserving his secrecy must be great indeed. During his career he has made public only something about his taste in authors. Although he refused to discuss contemporary figures, he did once tell William Maxwell that he loves "Kafka, Flaubert, Tolstoy, Chekhov, Dostoevsky, Proust, O'Casey, Rilke, Lorca, Keats, Rimbaud, Burns, E. Brontë, Jane Austen, Henry James, Blake, Coleridge."[47] As might be anticipated, the list is a mixture of devoted craftsmen and self-proclaimed seers, but with a preponderance of those preoccupied with the irrational. Except for the surprising inclusion of Jane Austen, the great intellectual satirists from Dante to George Bernard Shaw are conspicuously absent.

Although Salinger refused, on the occasion of listing his favorites, to discuss recent American writers, his fondness for Scott Fitzgerald and Ring Lardner are evident from frequent references to them in such works as "The Last Day of the Last Furlough" and *The Catcher in the Rye*. In "Zooey," Salinger's "alter ego" Buddy Glass even describes Fitzgerald's *The Great Gatsby* as his *Tom Sawyer*.[48] He has been even more sparing of adverse criticism of other authors, although he has Holden Caulfield speak disparagingly of Hemingway's *A Farewell to Arms* as "a phony book,"[49] and Buddy Glass near the beginning of "Seymour" lets off steam about the Beatniks and "all the bearded, proud, unlettered young men and unskilled guitarists and Zen-killers and incorporated aesthetic Teddy boys."[50] Salinger apparently has little use for the "red-blooded" school of fiction, as we might expect in view of his own preoccupation with finicky neurotics.

Despite all his efforts, though, Salinger cannot avoid being talked about, even preached about (at least at the Washington Square Methodist Church).[51] If, as reported, publicity disturbs Salinger, he is likely to be disturbed for some time to come.

"That David Copperfield Kind of Crap"

Leaving aside for the moment the question of the pleasure and value to be derived from Salinger's work, we can see even from the fragmentary knowledge we have of his life that he may serve as a cautionary example to those who, in their youthful pursuit of success, fail to realize that if the hard-to-please public does develop a rare enthusiasm for a writer, it may wish so to prolong the demonstration of its feelings that the artist becomes embarrassed and at last annoyed. If a writer really wishes to protect his privacy, he is likely to find it easier to take precautions before publishing his work (by writing, like Henry Green, for example, under a nom de plume) than after discovering that admirers can be a nuisance.

CHAPTER *2*

Phony and Nice Worlds

JUST AS one inspecting real estate must seek some promontory from which to get the lay of the land, the critic, trying to see an author's work in perspective, seeks some central document that provides a focal point from which the others may be viewed. Futhermore, since the work of any considerable writer is likely to exhibit a subtly varied surface that conceals a complex sub-surface structure rather than to be marked by a single conspicuous feature, more than one of his works may prove a useful starting point for organizing observations. So far comprehensive surveys of Salinger's work have begun with analyses of two distinguished short stories; I propose to utilize a third.

In view of the attention lavished upon Salinger during the decade that may go down in literary history as "the age of Holden Caulfield," there have been remarkably few critical surveys of all his writings. Most accounts have dealt only with *Catcher in the Rye* (and more recently with the stories of the Glass family), although Salinger's longest and most talked about work is not necessarily the most characteristic of his preoccupations. Two of the four writers of comprehensive studies—Ihab Hassan (*Radical Innocence*, 1961) and Paul Levine ("The Development of the Misfit Hero," *Twentieth Century Literature,* October, 1958)—examine the works chronologically in order to study Salinger's concentration upon a type of nonconformist that Levine labels "the misfit hero." Levine begins his account with Salinger's second published story, "The Hang of It," which concerns a soldier who marches out of step with his battalion; but he might as well have begun with the first, since William Jameson, Jr., in "The Young Folks," is as ill-at-ease in a sophisticated, predatory society as Holden Caulfield and most of

Salinger's other edgy adolescents. Hassan, writing of Salinger's fiction under the apt title "Rare Quixotic Gesture," traces from the beginning of the novelist's career a conflict between the "assertive vulgarian" and the "responsive outsider" who constantly attempts to reach out from his isolation. It is these "outsiders" who make the strange kind of "quixotic gesture" that "disrupts our habits of gray acquiescence and revives our faith in the willingness of the human spirit."[1]

A more complicated effort to classify Salinger's work is made in the first monograph about it, Frederick Gwynn and Joseph Blotner's *The Fiction of J. D. Salinger* (1958), which develops from an initial consideration of the poignant "For Esmé—with Love and Squalor." This first short book about Salinger, however, is criticism in the limited sense of the word; it is a rapid review of the author's works aimed at classifying and evaluating them rather than exhaustively analyzing them. The trouble with considering Salinger's other works in relation to "For Esmé" is that the story's superior artistic quality and its triumphantly affirmative conclusion cause one to look down from it as from an eminence rather than in different directions as from a watershed.

William Wiegand ("Seventy-Eight Bananas," *Chicago Review,* Winter, 1958), who approaches Salinger's work more objectively than Gwynn and Blotner, chooses "A Perfect Day for Bananafish"—the preface to the legend of the Glass family—as embodying an idea that had been embryonic even in Salinger's earliest stories. According to Wiegand, Salinger's major heroes have "banana fever," a spiritual illness characterized by the individual's inability either to distinguish between important and unimportant experiences or to realize that he cannot retain them all. Since these bananafish-heroes suffer keenly as a result of their lack of discrimination, their perfect day arrives, according to Wiegand, "when the bananafish is able to end all his sufferings by killing himself." This analysis, however, tends to stress the destruction of innocence in Salinger's work as strongly as Gwynn and Blotner's stresses the triumph of love. "A Perfect Day for Bananafish" and "For Esmé" are, in fact, the most successful embodiments so far of what might be called the manic and depressive extremes of Salinger's vision.

A study can move in both directions, however, only from a story that strikes a medium between these two—a story that ends in the triumph of neither love nor death but that depicts rather both the wonderful world of Esmé and the squalid world of Miami Beach from which Seymour escapes. Happily—since one could not assume that an artist who runs to extremes would ever pause to stake out a middle ground—Salinger has written just such a story: "Uncle Wiggily in Connecticut," one of the *Nine Stories* often grouped with the two already mentioned and with "Down at the Dinghy" as his most successful short works. Published in the *New Yorker* in 1948, the year that Salinger first won substantial recognition, this story has also the useful distinction of being the only one of Salinger's works to be filmed (or adapted with his consent for any other medium.)

I attach such importance to "Uncle Wiggily in Connecticut" because it is the only one of Salinger's works that offers, in a few pages, visions of both worlds with which he is concerned. I believe that these two worlds can best be distinguished by applying to them two adjectives that Salinger frequently uses—*nice* and *phony*. The "nice" world is that which we glimpse in the flashbacks in which Eloise recalls her idyllic days with Walt; the "phony" is that in which she now lives with her husband Lew. Nowhere in Salinger's writings is the contrast between these two worlds more tragically conjured up than in Eloise's final cry to her stone-drunk college chum, "I was a nice girl, wasn't I?"[2]

These contrasting worlds are epitomized in the title of the story: "Uncle Wiggily," borrowed by Walt from Howard Garis' children's stories about a whimsical rabbit and applied to the "nice" Eloise, is combined with "Connecticut," the chosen gathering place of the phony Madison Avenue exurbanites whom Holden Caulfield later rails against. It is significant that the "nice" part of the title is drawn from a work of fiction, while the "phony" part comes from a real place. Even the insignificant preposition "in" has an ominous overtone here, because it reminds the reader how much out of place "niceness" is in a "phony" world and stresses the triumph of the all-too-real Connecticut over the imaginary world of Uncle Wiggily. The story thus titled is the disquieting revelation of the change that has overtaken a person who is capable neither of the magnanimous gesture that lifts Esmé above her squalid surroundings nor of the impulsive action that releases Seymour Glass from his. Eloise has succumbed to the material comforts of the "phony" world and can now find only temporary relief from her despair in alcohol.

This only work of Salinger's to have been filmed so far appears to have been written with conversion to some dramatic medium in mind, for it almost perfectly illustrates the classical dramatic unities. The action takes place in a single afternoon in Eloise's living room—with only one climactic trip upstairs to her daughter's bedroom—and the action is almost exactly evenly divided between three scenes that are specifically announced as beginning at approximately three, five, and seven o'clock in the afternoon. In the first scene, we see Eloise as she is today; in the second, we learn what she has been in the past; in the third, we witness her sudden recognition of what has happened to her.

Of the two worlds contrasted in the story, the "phony" Connecticut is more vividly realized, as is essential since it is the one that really exists. The first paragraph of the story is a parade of adjectives hammering home the unpleasantness of the situation: Eloise's friend Mary Jane looks "fouled," the lunch is "burned," Mary Jane's employer has a hernia, and even the snow is "soiled." Lew, Eloise's pompous husband, who laughs only "at cartoons and stuff," symbolizes this world. He lied to Eloise when he told her that he admired Jane Austen; his favorite author is L. Manning Vines, the apparently imaginary author of a novel about four men's freezing to death in Alaska. Eloise supposes that he likes the story because the men die, thus satisfying Lew's sadistic impulses. We see this "phony" world at its most characteristic season—late winter, a time of frigid sterility. Nothing is created in this world. The maid's husband cannot spend the night with her. Although Eloise has only one wan child, her childless neighbors call her "fertile Fanny." This world is the "unreal city" of T. S. Eliot's *Waste Land*, the "valley of ashes" of Fitzgerald's *The Great Gatsby*.

Quite appropriately, the "nice" world that Eloise has lost is summoned up only fitfully when, in the first stages of drunkenness, she becomes maudlin. She glimpsed this world briefly when, as a dewy-eyed innocent from the Western wilderness who did not even dress like the New Yorkers, she met her lost lover Walt, who is not here identified as a member of the Glass family, but who has the same name, characteristics, and history as its only "lighthearted" son. He was the only boy who could make Eloise laugh; "he didn't try to be funny—he just *was* funny." She treasures the memory that once, when she twisted her ankle, Walt called it "Poor Uncle Wiggily." Another time, she recalls wistfully, he said that her stomach—which he was feeling with one hand—was so beautiful that, to be fair, he would like to be ordered to stick his other hand through a closed window. Surely this action would merit the term "rare, quixotic gesture" which Ihab Hassan applies to the behavior of Salinger's favored characters.

The loss of this "nice" world has turned Eloise into a bitch. Early in the story her present character is established when she refuses to agree that it is terrible that an old teacher wasted away to sixty-two pounds before dying of cancer. "You're getting hard as nails," Eloise's shocked ex-roommate says; but probably the thought of wasting away does not terrify the waste-lander. Just before Eloise begins to evoke the past, she executes "a grind and a bump," extraordinarily vulgar gyrations of the striptease dancer which serve both to symbolize her present coarseness and to foreshadow her "baring" of her emotional self in the next "act." In the third part of the story the tragic consequences of her degradation are disclosed. Drunk, she refuses to drive down the icy streets to meet her husband at the railroad station; completely callously—with a flippant remark about not keeping a hotel—she refuses to allow the maid's husband to stay overnight. Finally, when Eloise discovers that her introverted, myopic daughter has created another imaginary boy friend to replace one who has been "killed" (as Eloise's was really killed), she insists that the child destroy the illusion by moving to the center of the bed that she pretends to share. Then suddenly struck by the enormous cruelty of her behavior, Eloise sees the contrast between the happy past and the defiled present and rushes—without feeling the pain when she bruises her shin—over to a bedside table where she picks up her daughter's thick glasses, presses them against her tear-stained cheek, and cries "Poor Uncle Wiggily." The story ends when she goes back downstairs and asks her now sodden ex-roommate the question about having been a nice girl—the answer to which she both cherishes and fears.

We cannot quarrel with Gwynn and Blotner's conclusion that Eloise's "salvation-by-child" may be as "temporary" as Seymour

Glass's diversion from suicide by Sybil (if indeed he is really "diverted" at all); but their further claim that the ending of "Uncle Wiggily in Connecticut" is "abrupt" misses the point, for the story is not about Eloise's "salvation." Rather it is about her recognition of what has happened to her. She is like a character in Dante's Inferno who cannot escape but who has just discovered where he really is. Salinger contrasts two worlds and dramatizes the plight of the person who has the sensitivity to comprehend the "nice," whimsical world of the Glasses while possessing the toughness—which the Glasses generally lack—to endure in depraved Connecticut.

Why, however, is the "phony" world able to triumph over the "nice" world? "Uncle Wiggily in Connecticut" is further distinguished among Salinger's work because it is one of the few stories in which he ventures to answer the questions about the triumph of "phoniness" that so much distress Holden Caulfield. Many have lamented the worldly corruption of innocence. Some have placed the blame on human nature; others, on social institutions. Does Salinger embrace some kind of puritanical notion of original sin or does he embrace a Rousseauistic faith in a natural goodness that social institutions have corrupted? *The Catcher in the Rye* can be read—but not, I think, accurately —as an essay in support of the theory of natural goodness; but in his novel Salinger is, as I hope to demonstrate, concerned with the effects rather than the causes of the human predicament.

An answer to the question about the author's theories of man and the universe is provided, however, by "Uncle Wiggily in Connecticut," since it does picture, after her fall, a person who has once been "nice." Why couldn't Eloise remain in the "nice" world? If she or Walt had destroyed their chances by their own misdeeds, they would indeed serve as illustrations of human depravity, and Salinger would be linked to the puritanical tradition. If, on the other hand, Walt had been killed by enemy action—or even in line of duty—a savage society (what James Joyce calls an "old sow that eats her farrow") would be the culprit, and Salinger might be ranked among the Angry Young Rousseauists.

Walt, however, is killed neither by his own misdeeds nor by the deliberate malice of society. Eloise thus hysterically describes what did happen:

". . . his regiment was resting someplace. It was between battles or something, this friend of his said that wrote me. Walt and some other boy were putting this little Japanese stove in a package. Some colonel wanted to send it home. Or they were taking it *out* of the package to rewrap it—I don't know exactly. Anyway, it was all full of gasoline and junk and it exploded in their faces. The other boy just lost an eye."[3]

On the surface, the incident seems simply to have been a freak accident—an irrational or what an existentialist might call an "absurd" occurrence. Walt seems the victim neither of divine wrath nor of social injustice. Salinger's having him killed by accident in a rest camp rather than in action emphasizes the indifference of the universe to man's ideas of good and evil. The author seems here to embrace a notion much like that expressed in Stephen Crane's ironic little poem about man's existence creating no sense of obligation in the universe.[4] Man is simply at the mercy of the chaotic forces of blind chance. Another evidence that Salinger accepts the idea of an "absurd" universe is the senseless death from leukemia of Holden Caulfield's intelligent and likeable brother Allie.

"Uncle Wiggily in Connecticut" is not, however, just a simple elegy for man's helplessness in a world he never made. Eloise's account of Walt's death leaves some important questions unanswered—why were the soldiers packing or unpacking a stove full of gasoline? It is impossible to tell whether the Colonel—who probably acquired the stove as loot—or the young men themselves are responsible for this incredibly dangerous and stupid action. The ambiguity is surely quite deliberate. Salinger is pointing out, first, that somebody had been indifferent and irresponsible and, second, that the facts have not been ascertained. Walt was killed because somebody—possibly even he himself—had not taken the necessary safety precautions. Eloise's account foreshadows a curious passage in *The Catcher in the Rye* in which Holden comments on Jesus' disappointment in the disciples, whom He had to pick "at *random*" because "He didn't have time to go around analyzing everybody."[5] Holden is here obviously reading into Jesus' behavior his own failure to think things through before making important decisions. Things go wrong because people do not take the trouble to do them right.

Thus while Salinger does not Calvinistically thunder about special providences, he does at least implicitly accept the Puritan concept of man as a creature "depraved" in all his parts. Man does not retain his innocence, his "niceness," because he does not have the intelligence, the wisdom, or the foresight to retain it while attempting to meet the demands that the world makes upon him. Perhaps this view of man's inadequate capacity to serve both himself and society shows why Salinger feels that he must withdraw from society if he is to get his own work done. His withdrawal, however, is not like Thoreau's *Walden* "experiment." Rather Salinger is an "anti-transcendentalist," because he feels that man does not have the "self-reliance" to go serenely about his own business in the midst of distractions.

At least two more details from this story are important to a general consideration of Salinger's work. The thick, "counter-myopic" glasses that Eloise's daughter Ramona wears serve—like Raymond Ford's in "The Inverted Forest"—as evidence that the imaginatively gifted are often physically handicapped. In other stories like "Soft Boiled Sergeant" and "The Laughing Man," Salinger employs other variations on the Beauty and the Beast motif, although his refusal to believe that others are daring or intelligent enough to lift the spell from the Beast is further evidence of his vision of an indifferent universe peopled by men of drastically limited capacity. Whether from bitter personal experience, an inferiority complex, delusions of grandeur, or simply observation of others, Salinger is aware that internal and external beauty do not always accompany each other and that, since the insensitive world often perceives only exteriors, handsome hollow men flourish while physically handicapped but imaginative children suffer and are driven deeper into themselves.

Eloise's remark to Mary Jane (reminiscent of Doc's comments on the injudiciousness of telling the truth in the seventeenth chapter of John Steinbeck's *Cannery Row*) that it is inadvisable to tell one's husband the truth foreshadows Holden Caulfield's discovery at the end of *The Catcher in the Rye* that one cannot share his memories and retain his integrity. Although Uncle Wiggily may be domesticated, he remains a biting and scratching creature pining for his carefree life in the "nice" world.

Salinger apparently does not believe that there is any possible compromise between "niceness" and "phoniness." The acceptance of the "phony" world means compromising one's integrity. Salinger appears to have no concept of the kind of "autonomous" person whom David Riesman describes in *The Lonely Crowd* as "capable of conforming to the behavioral norms of society" but remaining free "to choose whether to conform or not"; in fact Salinger's writings almost directly contradict Riesman's thesis that "the individual is capable of more than his society usually asks of him."[6] The person who conforms either has as little sense of direction as Eloise's friend Mary Jane or retains only tearful memories of a nicer world.

That the story does present a contrast between two worlds was certainly overlooked by those responsible for "My Foolish Heart," the Samuel Goldwyn film based on this story and released in 1950. Although most reviewers found the motion picture superior to the common run (*Library Journal* called it "moving and thought-provoking" and *Time* dubbed it "a handsome production"), John McCarten, writing in the *New Yorker*, in which the story had originally appeared, found it full of "soap-opera clichés" and said that the script had certainly "done Mr. Salinger wrong."[7] McCarten's objections are justified. According to the summary in the *Motion Picture Herald* of the script devised by Julius and Philip Epstein, the film was unusually outspoken for a Hollywood production.[8] Yet it subverted Salinger's original in several ways.

These changes matter to a study of Salinger, not as fuel for controversy over the proper relationship between film and source but for the light that they throw on the effect of Salinger's story. Often we do not see the significance of an artist's handling of his material until we observe the different use another makes of it. These works are linked only by their setting and the names of the characters. In the film as in the story, an old friend visits Eloise's Connecticut home, and the past is revealed through flashbacks. In the film, however, Ramona proves to be the issue of premarital intimacies between Eloise and Walt, who was killed in a plane crash during the war. After hearing the news, the distraught Eloise had lured away and married the fiancé of the girl who is visiting her. When the picture begins, Eloise's marriage is on the rocks;

[44]

when it ends, the husband is departing with the other girl, leaving Eloise with the souvenirs of her blighted romance.

Three important differences between the story and the film script show the irreconcilability of Salinger's vision with the Epsteins' treatment of it. First, since in the film Eloise and Walt have engaged in premarital intercourse and since Eloise has stolen another girl's fiancé, Salinger's basic contrast between the "nice" and the "phony" worlds has vanished. In Salinger's terms, the Eloise of the film has been a calculating "phony" from the beginning. Second, Walt's death in line of duty makes him unequivocally the victim of a beast that devours its young. Salinger's careful working out of the ambiguity of the responsibility for the disaster is gone. Ironically, the film-makers have simplified the situation in just the way that Eloise says she would if she tried to explain it to her jealous and literalminded husband. Third, having Eloise's movie husband take off with his former fiancée turns the story into a conventional melodramatic account of the comeuppance of the erring hypocrite and the eventual reward of long-suffering virtue. In short, it is the story told from the viewpoint of all the "Connecticuts" in the world; but then, Samuel Goldwyn, of course, had to depend upon them to get his investment back.

The Epsteins and their colleagues turned a unique personal vision of the erosion of spontaneous innocence by a world of self-seeking "phonies" into a standard treatment of a formula incorporating the Old Testament concept of retributive justice. The real objection to this film—as to many "based" on literary works—is its use of the original author's name at all; it slights his talent to suggest that he may have been in any way responsible for a plot that any competent hack could have assembled from traditional, prefabricated materials.

Although strong meat for movie-goers (Roman Catholic critics complained that Eloise was not condemned strongly enough for her peccadilloes), the final triumph of "justice" at the end of "*My Foolish Heart*" strikes a conventionally optimistic note that serves by contrast to show just how despairingly pessimistic the writer of the original story was. "Uncle Wiggily in Connecticut" is actually not a dramatization of an ethical thesis at all; it is rather an almost appalling vision—like Frank Norris' *McTeague*—of man as an imperfect creature incapable of enough self-reliance to preserve his integrity and of civilization as a cage where the captive degenerates. As we shall see, these basic concepts of the perishability of the "nice" world and the "phoniness" of the persisting world provide the warp on which Salinger weaves with an increasingly deft hand the intricate, colorful patterns devised by the fancy of a conscientious craftsman.

CHAPTER *3*

The Old *Story*

FOR SEVENTEEN YEARS, through depression and war, Whit and Hallie Burnett provided through their magazine *Story* an outlet for works too unconventional for the slick magazines. Although most of the young writers they discovered have lapsed into obscurity, *Story* carried the first published short stories of such later celebrated writers as Norman Mailer, William Saroyan, Tennessee Williams, Truman Capote, and—perhaps most important of all—J. D. Salinger. Although Salinger began to break into the much more remunerative slicks like *Collier's* the year after his debut in *Story* in 1940, he continued to send the Burnetts those works that were too discomfiting for the widely circulated journals that specialized in tales of consoling escape.

His four contributions to *Story* have not been collected. While they lack the finesse of his better known fiction, it is unfair to dismiss them—as Gwynn and Blotner do in *The Fiction of J. D. Salinger*—as "arty sketches." They are important as examples of what he undoubtedly regarded as the most serious of his early work. Only the most astute critic could· have discerned in "The Young Folks," his first published story, the author who was to become the voice of a generation. Yet looking back at the story now, we can see that it might have been a rejected chapter for *The Catcher in the Rye*. Its principal figure, William Jameson, Jr., is a preliminary sketch of Holden Caulfield.

"The Young Folks" has hardly enough plot to be discussed as a story. The hostess at an amazingly decorous teen-age party introduces Jameson, who has been admiring from a distance a vivacious blonde attended by three Rutgers students, to Edna Phillips, who has been sitting unattended for three hours. Jameson, whose principal interest in life is biting his fingernails, wants to get a drink, but Edna has amorous notions. He tries to plead that he must go home to write a theme about Ruskin's *The Stones of Venice,* but Edna lures him to a darkened, outdoor terrace and attempts to rouse his jealous attentions by describing her pursuit by a sophisticated Princeton student. Jameson fails to respond, however, and retreats into the house. Edna then ventures into a part of the house forbidden to the "young folks" in order to pilfer some cigarettes and returns to imply to the hostess that young Jameson—who has rejoined the group of admirers surrounding the blonde—has made some crude romantic advances toward her.

Since both young people are unattractively doltish, readers of the early 1940's must have found it difficult to tell where—if anywhere—the author's sympathies lay. Looking back on the story with *The Catcher in the Rye* ineradicably impressed upon our minds, we realize that Edna's twice using the word "grand," which Holden Caulfield especially despises, should be added to her other crimes of pilfering cigarettes, cattily pointing out that her good-natured rival has bleached hair, and fabricating romantic adventures with the retarded Jameson. All these are evidence that she is a "phony," while young Jameson's innocent desire to admire gay young ladies from a distance but not to engage in passionate pastimes is a sign of gallantry. Just how a psychiatrist might interpret the action of the young swain who throws peanuts down the back of the attractive blonde would be interesting to know.

The inexperience of the author of "The Young Folks" is shown by his addiction to the kind of "colorful" language that creative writing teachers encourage; characters in this story are described as "yodeling hellos," as "swishing" rather than walking, as "knitting what there was of her brows," as "huskying" through the refrain of a song. Salinger had yet to develop his famous ear for the nuances of teen-age talk. Like much apprentice writing, the story could be dismissed if Salinger's nail-gnawing hero were not so patently a prototype of Holden Caulfield, and Edna Phillips the model for the patronizing, prevaricating "phonies" that make Holden's life miserable. Blotner and Gwynn completely miss the point of this story when they assume that Edna is a pathetic character and that Jameson is stupid rather than innocent. Certainly their statement that Edna retires near the end of the story "presumably to cry" rather than to replenish her supply of cigarettes needs amendment. An adolescent vamp, she is drawn, I suspect, not from life but from Salinger's childhood memories of actresses like Theda Bara.

Mention of Theda Bara is relevant to Salinger's other contributions to *Story*, for all deal with characters who—not without cause—some time in their life prefer the movies to real life, and the evasion of reality is the theme that ties together these three discomfiting tales.

"The Long Debut of Lois Taggett," which the Burnetts singled out for anthologizing, is artistically the least impressive of Salinger's contributions to *Story*. The tale of Miss Taggett focuses upon an empty-headed and self-centered Manhattan society girl whose vanity cannot cope with the blow it receives when her psychotic first husband smashes a lit cigarette into her hand and crushes her foot with a golf club. Since the husband is made of sterner stuff than is Seymour Glass, the unhappy union ends in divorce, not suicide; and he even masochistically attempts to win Lois back after receiving psychiatric treatment.

Instead of encouraging him, however, Lois enters into a loveless marriage with Carl Curfman, "who always wore white socks because colored socks irritated his feet." Driven into marriage—like James Purdy's Malcolm—because she cannot think of anything else to do, Lois turns into the same kind of bitch as Eloise in "Uncle Wiggily in Connecticut." She denies Carl the simple pleasures he enjoys and insists that he wear colored socks. Up to the point—almost at the end of the story—at which Lois introduces her baby to his father and Carl ruefully observes that the boy doesn't know him from Adam, the story, outlining the degeneration of a girl without wit enough to think for herself in an irrationally cruel world, seems a rough draft for "Uncle Wiggily in Connecticut." In the last four paragraphs, however, Salinger reduces the story to soap-opera by having Lois, after her baby smothers in its sleep, inexplicably turn into the kind of girl people admire and like to do things for. We would suppose that such a traumatic experience would have made Lois more bitter and vindictive than she had been, but her reform, which is evidently the conclusion of her long debut into true maturity, is symbolized by her last words in the story: they grant her husband permission to go back to wearing white socks only.

Although this story has the most affirmative ending of any that Salinger was to write until nearly a decade later when he produced "For Esmé—with Love and Squalor" and although Lois' gesture of unselfish love foreshadows Franny's joy at the end of the more celebrated "Zooey," the ending of "The Long Debut" distresses rather than impresses, for there is nothing that either logically leads up to it or renders it credible. Perhaps Lois has become one of those characters who has finally "made it," but we have only Salinger's word for it. The ending is imposed upon the story rather than developed from it. The difference between the "revelation" here and in "Uncle Wiggily in Connecticut" is that Eloise is shown as having at least two sides to her character—she possesses the sensitivity to comprehend Walt's whimsical world as well as the toughness to endure in depraved Connecticut. Lois Taggett, on the other hand, has throughout the story displayed only one kind of behavior and has never even demonstrated the imagination necessary to conceive of another. It is difficult to imagine how a sudden revelation could change a person's basic pattern of behavior rather than merely redirect her efforts ("converts" usually just work with their previous intensity toward some different end).

More convincing than the ending of "The Long Debut of Lois Taggett" is Salinger's earlier description of Lois driven by the boredom of her second marriage into constantly going to the movies—as early as eleven o'clock in the morning—because living in the fantasy world of the films was better than sitting at home, visiting her nagging mother, or gossiping with other girls. Salinger succeeds far better than Walker Percy in the novel entitled *The Movie-Goer* (1961) in drawing a portrait of the frustrated American whose efforts to evade not only mature responsibility but even recognition of the evasion result in compulsive movie-going. Salinger's deep interest in this too-common type of person is also illustrated by his last two contributions to *Story.*

In "Once a Week Won't Kill You," the most sentimental of the group, the movie-goer is Aunt Rena, a woman in her early fifties at the time of World War II, whose life apparently really ended when a second lieutenant in World War I failed—for unspecified reasons—to return to her. Since then she has consoled herself by listening to the radio and being shepherded to the movies, while living more and more in her dream of the past.

As the story opens, the nephew with whom she lives is getting ready to enter the army. His principal regret is that this woman who worries about being fair to radio advertisers will have to be told he is leaving, for he wishes her to be "the one woman in 1944 who did not have someone's hour-glass to watch." He has no visible regrets about leaving his ambitious wife, who wishes him to maneuver for a commission and to be stationed in London so that he can send her some tweed. Although they have been married three years, the wife still talks to him in "italics." Despite all she wishes from him, he finds it difficult to extract from her the single promise that she will continue to take his aunt to the movies once a week.

The disruptions caused by war are always distressing, but what is annoying about this story is the sympathy that Salinger tries to drum up for the distress that calling a man into the service may cause a woman who has been out of touch with reality for a quarter of a century. We cannot share the nephew's fears that even his departure will give her "an hour-glass" that Aunt Rena will consciously watch. War causes enough painful shattering of illusions to make worry over the shattering of delusions appear to be rampant sentimentality. Salinger attempts in this story to arouse sympathy for a man whose desire to arrest the passage of time is nearly as psychotic as his aunt's dwelling in the past. The man's gallant efforts to preserve his aunt's delusion foreshadow, of course, Holden Caulfield's ambitions to be a catcher in the rye. Holden, however, remains enough in touch with reality to recognize wistfully that he must relinquish his quixotic ambition. The principal character in "Once a Week Won't Kill You," appears irredeemable, and the story is simply pointlessly depressing.

By far the best and the most genuinely moving of Salinger's contributions to *Story* is "Elaine," which concerns not one, but three compulsive movie-goers. The title character's preference for movies over reality, however, is entirely justified; she is an extremely beautiful moron who takes nine and a half years to get through grammar school and even then has no idea of what it is in girls that interests boys. Her mother and maternal grandmother are just enough more intelligent to live on insurance proceeds, to read movie ads, and to warn her cryptically against allowing men to get "funny" with her, without specifying what they mean by "funny."

Elaine's mental deficiency, however, is her protection against male wiles: although she "was not unwilling to go out with boys . . . she was unwilling to be confused by unfamiliar, evadable issues." She is forced to face the issue, however, when at sixteen she is invited to the nearby beach—her first trip there—by an effeminate movie usher who constantly combs his thin hair. Although Elaine experiences "a terrible panic" when he asks her to walk beneath the boardwalk with him, he, employing what Salinger editorially describes as "the eternal rake's despicable but seldom faulty intuition," apparently finds Elaine a pushover to seduce. Although Salinger does not specify what happens—he has always had an aversion, extraordinary among contemporary writers, to the mention of the occurrence of sexual intercourse—Elaine and the usher Teddy (Salinger seems to favor this name for intuitive young men) are married only a month later.

The marriage is never legally consummated, however, because Elaine's mother, wakening for one critical moment to reality, forces the girl to abandon her husband and—despite his threats of obtaining an annulment—carries her off once again to the safe world of what the mother calls "a nice movie." As Elaine's gladiola wedding corsage fades and dies, she chooses to go to a Henry Fonda movie. Presumably it is more pleasant to live in the imaginary world of apparently virile Henry Fondas who cannot actually lay hands upon one than to live in the real world of effeminate Teddys with quarrelsome mothers and lecherous ideas. In this story, however, Salinger convinces the reader that it is indeed better both for those as feebly mentally endowed as the Cooneys and for society in general if such people spend their time attending movies rather than grappling with the problems of real life.

Because "Elaine" has not been reprinted, critics have not given it the attention it deserves as evidence of the ideas underlying Salinger's work. Since he expresses few value judgments in his early stories, we are rarely given the insight into his attitudes provided by the vicious characterization of the sexually aggressive movie usher, who, while immoral, seems not an unusual representative of his time and place.

The seemingly contradictory picture of this boy as at once

effeminate and an "eternal rake" indicates—as does the sympathetic presentation of young Jameson's rebuff of the vamp in "The Young Folks" and Lois Taggett's hysterical repulse of an amorous ranch-hand in Reno—that young Salinger became almost irrational at the idea of promiscuity. His picture of the happy community of three generations of modern idol-worshippers after Elaine's father drops dead at an indoor flea circus and of the women's discourteous responses to the attentions of the naïve superintendent of their apartment house can hardly be interpreted as anything except praise for the superiority of the life spent in the darkness of the theatre rather than the love nest. Indeed Elaine, her mother, and her grandmother appear to be modern nuns cloistered in the cinema, and Salinger satirizes everything about their seedy society except their worship of movie stars.

Gywnn and Blotner, who mention "Elaine" only to suggest that it resembles the works of James T. Farrell, miss altogether the point that the girl's mother does not whisk her "home," but out of the arms of her flesh-and-blood husband into the temple of a two-dimensional god who will never violate her. Other critics have failed either to search out the story or to understand that it may throw light upon critical episodes of *The Catcher in the Rye* and of *Franny and Zooey*, in both of which characters are literally sickened at the thought of sex.

CHAPTER 4

Slick Stuff

I A *"Short, Short"* Trail

HARDLY MORE than a year after his professional debut, Salinger made the big time. In the "good old days" before television, more than two dozen magazines offered generous rewards for "short, short stories"—usually less than a thousand words in length and building up to a surprise ending in the O. Henry manner. Salinger moved directly from *Story* to *Collier's*, one of the best paying publishers of "short, shorts." The two variations on the same "suppressed identity" gimmick that Salinger sold to *Collier's* deserve notice for three reasons. They show: first, that he could—if he wished—write "slick" fiction employing hackneyed formulas; second, that he did not long "blush unseen"; and, third, that he has a knack for constructing "well-made" stories. As artless as some of his tales appear, he can carefully plan to achieve certain effects if he so desires.

"The Hang of It," the earlier of the "short, shorts" is little more than an exercise in structure. A series of loosely related episodes showing a tough army sergeant's displeasure with a butterfingered World War I recruit are tied together by the repeated refrain: Sergeant, "Ain'tcha got no brains?" Recruit, "I'll get the hang of it." At the end of the story the recruit turns out to have become the commander of the regiment in which the same exasperated (but enduring) sergeant is having trouble with the commander's butterfingered son. "Personal Notes of an Infantryman" is about an army volunteer who gives up a defense plant foremanship when his son is wounded and insists upon being sent abroad for combat duty despite his age and family obligations. At the end, the army recruiting officer who narrates the story proves to be the volunteer's other son.

This brief fantasy about a middle-aged "catcher in the rye" marks Salinger's first use in print of the word millions would later regard as his trademark—"phony." When trying to decide how to console his mother about his father's going overseas, the narrator with the cushy job considers telling her that the older man was "gallant," but he decides that "the allusion was learned and phony." He then rejects some other terms as also "on the long-haired side." Much about Salinger's notion of "phoniness" and his preference for narrators who speak colloquially is suggested by the association that he makes between "phoniness" and the phrase "long-haired," so often used contemptuously to describe nonconformists dedicated to serious art. We might expect such an equation from a writer who is trying to disassociate himself from conspicuously dedicated artists and to associate himself chummily with the "general reader," whom Salinger addresses at such length at the beginning of "Seymour: An Introduction," his most recent story.

The narrator of "Personal Notes of an Infantryman" is also the first of Salinger's many "evaders." Eliot Fremont-Smith, in his review of *Franny and Zooey*, points out that in Salinger's world "nobody deals with anyone *directly*."[1] His characters are always talking over telephones or from behind shower curtains. The inability to face another person directly is not peculiar, however, to Salinger's recent creations. "I had to avoid his eyes," the narrator of "Personal Notes" says in describing an interview with his father; "I don't know quite why." Like many successors in Salinger's fiction, he simply could not look directly at another person and tell him what he thought.

People thus embarrassed to the point of inarticulateness provide the link between this story and Salinger's first contribution to *Esquire*, also published in 1941. Labeled a "satire," "The Heart of a Broken Story" parodies the kind of short, boy-meets-girl story that *Collier's* favored. After theorizing about the difficulties a shy young man would have becoming acquainted with a girl that he saw on a bus and fell in love with at first sight (the same kind of girl Holden Caulfield says he likes in "I'm Crazy"), Salinger concludes that the unlikeliness of romance blossoming from such a start is the reason he never writes boy-meets-girl stories.

Yet this awkwardly told tale is—despite the author's disclaimer —a boy-meets-girl story. Although Justin Horgenschlag does not meet the girl with the slightly parted lips whom he admires on the bus, he does meet Doris Hillman, "who was beginning to be afraid she wasn't going to get a husband." Actually the "satire" is a crude prototype of the deft "Uncle Wiggily in Connecticut." Like Eloise, Justin is doomed by fickle fate and his own inadequacy to seize his chance at entering the "nice" world of slick romance, so that he must settle for the drab security of "fouled" reality. What Salinger really means at the end of this story is that he could not write *dream*-boy-meets-*dream*-girl stories because—despite what popular songs tell us—two dreams never do meet.

II *Some Old School Tries*

Ironically, Salinger himself was a victim of the universe's indifference when he was denied the chance to have published as early as 1941 or 1942 a story in what was to become his best-loved vein. The *New Yorker* had purchased "Slight Rebellion Off Madison," an early installment in the Holden Caulfield saga, in 1941, but did not publish it because of America's entry into World War II. In the meantime Salinger—himself drafted into the service—cast about, principally in the pages of the *Saturday Evening Post,* for a satisfactory means of expressing himself artistically. His first three *Post* contributions, vastly different in style and content, are obviously the works of a man groping to find a path worth pursuing. In the fourth, he stumbles at last upon the track that will lead directly to "A Perfect Day for Bananafish" and the final version of *The Catcher in the Rye.*

Salinger broke into the *Post* with "The Varioni Brothers" (July 17, 1943), his initial attempt to come up with a statement about the role of the artist in modern American society. Gwynn and Blotner complain in *The Fiction of J. D. Salinger* that it is impossible to tell who or what this Fitzgeraldesque story is about; but their protest appears the result of their looking for too much complexity in a superficial and straightforward yarn. The week before printing "The Varioni Brothers," the editors of the *Post* summed up the fable quite adequately as "the moving story of two brothers who were geniuses and of how one of them used and thwarted the genius of the other."

The story is a thinly disguised morality play about a problem that has constantly bothered artists in a materialistic society: should one settle for commercial success or labor over a great work of art that may go unnoticed? Joe Varioni is one of those rare souls who can write either enormously successful lyrics for popular songs or fiction of supreme artistic value. His brother Sonny, on the other hand, is a song-writer who knows only the art of suiting the public taste. Playing the devil's advocate, Sonny prevails upon Joe to give up the novel he is writing on match-folders in order to devote his time to grinding out *kitsch*. When the money begins to roll in, Sonny thwarts Joe's efforts to return to his job as a college teacher and to his neglected novel; but Sonny also becomes bored with easy success and becomes involved with notorious gamblers. A hench-man of one of these racketeers kills Joe, whom he mistakes for Sonny. The surviving brother thereupon disappears for seven-teen years and finally returns, a broken man, to the college where Joe taught. He is determined to devote the little that is left of his life to trying to put together the fragments of Joe's novel. He has discovered that he really hears "music" for the first time when he reads this book, although during his days of commercial success he had scoffed at Joe's stories as ones in which nothing happened.

The reason that Sonny had earlier refused to let Joe return home comes to light when Sonny asks the girl who begs him to set his brother free: "What makes you so sure he wouldn't plug out words for years and then have a bunch of guys tell him he was also-ran?" Any artist might face the same problem. Why should he run the risk of passing up easy money to devote his time to producing an ambitious work that might be scorned? It is especially ironic, however, that the question underlying this morale-building tale should obviously have so much troubled the man who was to write the outstandingly successful American novel of the postwar period. Salinger has evidently been more concerned about critical reaction to his work than he has cared to admit directly.

"The Varioni Brothers," which Salinger hoped the movies might buy, in several ways remarkably resembles the author's most recently published work, "Seymour: An Introduction." Both are sympathetic portrayals of talented college English instructors, and both depict a man whose primary concern in life has become the preparation for public presentation of the remarkable remains of his dead brother's unacknowledged genius. Finally, both of these geniuses are lovable eccentrics who have been destroyed prematurely by an insensitive world. The significance of these similarities is that, in his most recent work, Salinger appears not to be exploring new areas of experience but working over pious visions that he has long entertained.

"The Varioni Brothers" also sheds light—through Joe's girl's violent denunciation of the "high, wide, and rotten twenties"— on a curious passage in *The Catcher in the Rye* in which Holden labels Hemingway's Lt. Henry in *A Farewell to Arms* "a phony" while praising Scott Fitzgerald's Gatsby.[2] The seemingly inexplicable attack upon Hemingway's extremely individualistic hero is puzzling until we recall that there is little approval anywhere in Salinger's writing for those who enjoy sexual intercourse out of wedlock, reject the world, make "a separate peace," and do not allow the unfeeling world to defeat or destroy them. Gatsby, on the other hand, after creating his Long Island "dream world" is amazingly circumspect in his relations with Daisy and does allow himself to be destroyed rather than abandon his dream. Salinger's characters seem to agree with Nick Carraway that Gatsby is "worth the whole damn bunch put together," and the narrator of "The Varioni Brothers" even uses the very adjective that Nick Carraway does when speaking generally of the "successful" people of the 1920's as "a rotten crowd."[3]

Certainly Staff-Sergeant Salinger was not prepared to make "a separate peace" in the mid-1940's. Regardless of the edifying conclusion of "The Varioni Brothers," Salinger continued to grind out for the slicks the fodder that sentimentalists thrive upon. About the most trivial of all his stories is "Both Parties Concerned," the tearful idyll of a couple who married too young. The husband-father does not want to accept his responsibilities; so he leaves the baby with a sitter and takes his wife out partying every night after his hard days at the aircraft factory. When she finally leaves him, an evening of solitary drinking convinces him that he must indeed "grow out of certain things" and find "a new kind of fun." Like Lois Taggett in a similar story, he "makes it," as the reader learns when he tells his wife, whom he has won back from her officious mother, to wake him up whenever the thunder frightens her. Although his transformation is more completely accounted for than Lois', it is no more convincing; it occurs with remarkable rapidity and under the influence of alcohol.

For his third *Post* story, Salinger returned to the military scenes with which he was now becoming personally familiar. "Soft Boiled Sergeant," however, is perhaps the most sentimental of all his stories. The title character, Sergeant Burke, has managed to remain through years of military service "the catcher in the rye" that Holden Caulfield only longs to be. Burke's character is revealed by his allowing the homesick young soldier who later tells the story to wear a chestful of the sergeant's decorations—including "the highest"—on his underwear until the young man becomes accustomed to barracks life. Despite his nobility, Burke is ugly and has an unbecoming "two-toned" voice, so that the kind of pretty, shapely girl he admires shuns him. He must go through life an unredeemed prince in the guise of a beast because no beauty will dare to kiss him. He finally loses his life rescuing three scared young soldiers during the attack on Pearl Harbor.

The purpose of the story is not, however, to eulogize Burke, but to offer advice to prospective husbands. The narrator's point is that one should shy away from the kind of girl who avoids Burke and marry only the kind that cries when she hears his story. A second purpose is to criticize most movies about army life as unrealistic because their heroes are too superficially glamorous. Whether Salinger's variation of "Beauty and the Beast" is any more realistic than Hollywood's concept of war is, however, debatable. Salinger was well aware that a charming exterior might cover a spiritual void, but it seems never to have occurred to him that the same could be true of an ugly exterior. One does not make something new simply by turning the old inside out.

III A Babe That Came and Went

If Salinger had produced only such light-weight fabrications as "Both Parties Concerned" and "Soft Boiled Sergeant," he would never have had much impact upon the public. But with his fourth contribution to the *Post*, he began publishing those stories that would endear him to readers above all other authors to emerge from World War II. The Varioni brothers and Sergeant Burke had existed only for the purpose of delivering a single questionable message; but with the creation of Babe

Gladwaller and his friends, Salinger began to write of characters who moved from one adventure to another in a fictional world that seemed increasingly more real and that excited and perplexed readers could identify with their own.

"The Last Day of the Last Furlough" is one of the best of Salinger's uncollected stories. Although its sentimental style cloys upon repeated readings, the story is a remarkably effective evocation of the disturbed feelings of an unsophisticated soldier during his last day at home before being shipped overseas—possibly to his death. Salinger succeeds in producing in this story the kind of dramatic transcript of a critical day in a man's life that many soldier-authors fumbled toward.

Babe Gladwaller, the soldier in the story, is the first Salinger character to play the leading role in a series of related tales. He is a kind of cross between Holden Caulfield and Buddy Glass. Steadier (he did become a technical sergeant), better mannered, and more conventionally literary than Holden, he shares the boy's fondness for small children and other spontaneous innocents and his embarrassment about displaying his true feelings. Less sophisticated and ironic than Buddy, he is also a withdrawn literary man with a penchant for rereading favorite books (including, as we might by now anticipate in a Salinger story, *The Great Gatsby*) and old family letters. Unlike most Salinger characters, he is still—although in his twenties—extremely deferential toward his father, a garrulous college professor in Valdosta, New York.

On this crucial day the reader meets him wearing civilian clothes (in violation of wartime military regulations), drinking milk that it is too often emphasized is "ice-cold," and reacquainting himself with *Anna Karenina* and *The Brothers Karamazov*, among other Salinger props. He abandons his beloved books to take a sled to the school where he will meet his ten-year-old sister Mattie. She is late because the teacher is reading *Wuthering Heights* after class to a small band of devotees. As Babe fervently hopes, Mattie wants Cathy to marry Heathcliffe instead of Linton. On the way home, Babe—in the irrational manner of many of Salinger's child-fanciers—torments Mattie until she desperately agrees to sled down a dangerous street with him as a sign of her trust in him. When she capitulates, he relents, and they pursue a less dangerous road home, where they find a friend of Babe's, twenty-nine-year-old Vincent Caulfield. Babe is delighted when the whimsical Vincent—who in civilian life writes soap operas—charms Mattie in a conversation reminiscent of that between Seymour Glass and Sybil in "A Perfect Day for Bananafish."

At dinner, Babe breaks into his father's rambling reminiscences of World War I with a passionate statement about his belief in the aims of World War II and his more urgent hope that men in the future will feel that it is their "moral duty" not to reminisce about the war. Young men, he fears, are misled by such reminiscences into believing that war is romantic. Instead of sticking to his guns, though, Babe suddenly becomes "afraid that he had made a terrible fool of himself" before his father and Vincent. That night, the two young men go out with Babe's girl friends. Vincent tells him—as Babe had hoped he wouldn't—that the smart, pretty, steady girl Babe allowed Vincent to escort is worth ten of the other; but Babe is attracted by the very whimsicality, unreliability, and silly affectation—in short, the childishness—of the other. Home from his date, he goes into the room where Mattie is sleeping and, without waking her, hopes aloud that she may grow up to be a "swell girl." She awakens and forces him to confess that he is being shipped overseas although he does not wish his mother to find out. His mother, however, also wakes up and guesses the truth.

What the story principally depicts, however, is not Babe's effort to conceal the truth so that no depressing clouds blight his last day in this world of familiar pleasures, but the desperate and unavailing effort of a shy and sensitive young man to hold on to his irresponsible and carefree youth in the face of irresistible forces that are compelling him to accept adult responsibilities. Babe's addiction to ice-cold milk and chocolate cake, his close identification with his ten-year-old sister, his embarrassment when he discusses adult matters seriously in adult company, and his preference for his childish sweetheart, are all evidences of an irrational attempt to cling to both the physical and intellectual innocence that the ostensibly wise and rational forces of maturity seem bent upon destroying—just as they have destroyed the lives of the young men whom they have led to romanticize war. Since Salinger is intent in this story upon capturing this brief, futile passion for innocence rather than upon conveying a message, "The Last Day of the Last Furlough" is one of those unusually moving artistic works that seem not to *mean* but to *be*. The story depicts not a crisis in the life of Everyman, but the inner feelings of those who prefer to dwell in the "nice" world of their imaginations rather than in the "phony" world of sad partings.

Salinger was evidently satisfied enough with the characters in "The Last Day of the Last Furlough" to write of them again. The sequels, however, fail to measure up to the original. Part of the trouble may be simply that they are so much shorter and less complex than the first story that they appear to be only appendages to it. The more serious trouble, however, is that the attachment of a soldier to his young sister, which had seemed touching in "The Last Day of the Last Furlough," becomes a morbid preoccupation when it persists past the occasion that legitimately prompted it. We can sympathize with a soldier about to be shipped overseas who attempts pathetically to cling to his childish innocence by seeking the affection of a child; but when he continues to dream in a battlefield foxhole, from which he has just removed the bloody remains of a dead enemy, about this same little sister and when he later takes her along to visit a dead buddy's ex-girl friend, we begin to feel that his sentiments approach those that Vladimir Nabokov exploits and satirizes in *Lolita*.

"A Boy in France," the second story about Babe Gladwaller, is hard to justify except as the kind of exercise in sheer sentimentality that one might expect it to be upon discovering that the "boy" of the title is an army sergeant in his twenties. As in "The Last Day of the Last Furlough," there is no plot, but neither is there—as there is in the previous story—a complex exploration of ambivalent feelings. There is only a record of discontent and discomfort. Salinger follows in harrowing detail the steps by which Babe painfully installs himself for the night in a foxhole dug by a German presumably dead. We are distressed that any human beings must live even temporarily under such conditions, but Babe does not reflect—like Sergeant X in "For Esmé—with Love and Squalor"—upon either his dehumanization or the absurdities of human behavior that have caused it. Instead he worries about a lost fingernail and dirty underwear, scowls at a supercilious Broadway columnist's report of home front hi-jinks, and finally lulls himself to sleep rereading a letter in which ten-year-old Mattie laments the shortage of boys at the beach. Rather than stressing the singular plight of the soldier in an alien land, the story reduces war to an outing by a group of inept Boy Scouts and makes Babe into a lazy tenderfoot mooning over his puppy love.

"A Boy in France" was Salinger's last contribution to the *Post*. Babe Gladwaller, home from the war, turned up next in *Collier's* in "The Stranger," a story in which there is no real relationship between the parts. It describes Babe's hauling the still-not-very-much-matured Mattie along to visit the ex-girl friend of Vincent Caulfield, who has been killed during the war by a mortar barrage. The high point of the story is Babe's impassioned speech against the injustice done every girl whose lover has been killed by a mortar shell that he did not hear coming. Unfortunately, this speech has no relationship to Vincent or to his ex-girl friend because they had broken up before he went overseas, and she had already married another man before Vincent died.

In fact, the girl's explanation of their break is that Vincent had not believed in anything since the time before the war when his younger brother Kenneth had died.[4] Just why the death of a younger brother should alienate a man from his girl friend is not explained. Vincent—like characters in some nineteenth-century sentimental romances—seems to have been withdrawing altogether from a world that had destroyed the innocent child he loved; but then the mortar barrage has had nothing to do with the break between the lovers. It seems simply to have ended abruptly and somewhat mercifully a tragedy that has already passed its climax. Since the story fails to be either a satisfactory anti-war preachment or an explanation of the really central question of why Vincent's relationship with the woman he loves is not enough to counteract his grief over the death of a sibling, "The Stranger" can only be judged one of Salinger's most complete failures.

With this story Babe Gladwaller disappears from Salinger's work. Probably there was nothing more to say about him. The war had not altered him either physically or mentally; and, if war could not change him, it is not likely that much else could. We see him for the last time admiring his sister Mattie's jumping from the curb as a mystifyingly "beautiful thing to see," and we are left with the impression that he is likely to spend the rest of his life looking with longing incomprehension at light-hearted children. He is a "catcher in the rye" who has "made it." Little more can be said about life in his private kindergarten unless an ill-advised marriage to his silly, affected sweetheart drives him to share the fate of Seymour Glass. As William Wiegand points out, Babe has "an incipient case of banana fever." "A Perfect Day for Bananafish" thus may provide not only an opening chapter for the Glass saga, but a possible conclusion to the story of Babe Gladwaller.

IV *The First Holden Caulfield*

One of the things that is most likely to interest readers in "The Last Day of the Last Furlough" is Vincent Caulfield's distress because he has just received word that his brother Holden, who used to be the "noisiest, toughest kid" in a New York bar favored by prep schoolers, is missing in action. Apparently this is the fate that Salinger intended for the Holden Caulfield who appeared in the short story that was sold in 1941 to the *New Yorker*. Questions about whether this is the "same" Holden as the one in the final version of *The Catcher in the Rye* can really only be answered by saying that, after the war, Salinger decided to revive his character and completely revamp his biography. Even Holden's family is not the same in "The Last Day of the Last Furlough" and *The Catcher in the Rye*. Although Holden's older brother in the novel, D. B., is not much different from Vincent, Holden's parents in the novel are not actors, as they are in several stories written during the war.

Even before publishing the last of the three Babe Gladwaller stories, Salinger had begun to move the Caulfields to the center of the stage in "This Sandwich Has No Mayonnaise," published in *Esquire*. As Gwynn and Blotner have pointed out, the weakness of this story is that halfway through it, the interest inexplicably shifts from Vincent Caulfield, who finds too many soldiers on a truck that is taking the men to a dance, to a lieutenant who solves the problem of what to do about the extra men. If we are to share Vincent's depression over the news that his brother Holden is missing in action, he should remain the center of interest in the story. Gwynn and Blotner do not bring out, however, all the reasons why the story is irritating rather than moving.

The obscured truth of the matter is that, if Vincent is really responsible for loading the truck, he is also responsible for checking the rosters to see that the proper men are on board. He has failed, however, to do his job—just as he has failed to keep track of a raincoat containing some treasured letters. Yet even though he is at fault, he is unwilling to relinquish his own place in the group, as he could after the lieutenant arrives. In short, Vincent is so upset about Holden's being missing in action that he cannot do his duty properly; yet he is determined to go to the dance, where he will probably make others miserable. All the small-talk between the men in the truck that makes up much of the story is not padding; it emphasizes the world's indifference to Vincent's plight. The rather perverse point of the end of the story (the lieutenant calls up a girl he knows and makes her come to the dance through the rain) is that Vincent's suffering will be in some way mitigated or at least compensated for, if someone else is inconvenienced.

The story falls apart because Salinger wishes the reader to sympathize with Vincent and cannot, therefore, expose him as both the culprit of the piece and the victim of a monstrous self-pity. Readers unfamiliar with military routine would miss—as critics have—the point that Vincent is responsible for the mess that the officer has to straighten out; but, unless the reader realizes that Vincent is responsible, there is no connection between the confusion over who should be on the truck and Vincent's agony over Holden. Because Salinger cannot play fair with both the reader and his character, the story of how the officer solves the problem of who should attend the dance and the harrowing description of Vincent's despair seem parallel accounts awkwardly yoked together rather than closely related parts of a sentimentally biased presentation of irresponsible behavior.

So far Holden Caulfield had appeared only in the conversation and memories of other characters. In "I'm Crazy" (*Collier's*, December 22, 1945), he emerged at last as a character in his own right. A year later, he was heard of again when the long deferred "Slight Rebellion Off Madison" at last appeared in the *New Yorker*. Both stories offer earlier versions of material incorporated into *The Catcher in the Rye*. "I'm Crazy" is in two scenes: the first, Holden's interview with his history teacher before his flight from his preparatory school; the second, his conversation with Phoebe in her bedroom. "Slight Rebellion Off Madison" describes Holden's theatre date with Sally Hayes.

A comparison of these stories with the passages in *The Catcher in the Rye* in which some of the same material is used gives some idea of the manner in which the story of Holden Caulfield evolved over a ten-year period. Salinger had apparently been working on it since he had begun to write with an eye to publication. He told Shirley Blaney that his "boyhood was very much the same as that of the boy in the book" and that he "was much relieved" when he finished "telling people about it."[5] His first published story, "The Young Folks," is about a young man much like Holden, whose brush with a pseudo-sophisticated girl might have been used in *The Catcher in the Rye*. As has been pointed out, he sold the original version of "Slight Rebellion Off Madison" to the *New Yorker* in 1941. Just how this version may have differed from the one finally published cannot be told, but Salinger certainly revised it after the war, since the play which is mentioned in it, "O Mistress Mine," did not open in New York until February, 1946. Curiously "Random Harvest," which Gwynn and Blotner identity in *The Fiction of J. D. Salinger* as the movie described in *The Catcher in the Rye*, was the Christmas feature at the Radio City Music Hall in 1942. When Salinger got around to finally revising the story, he rewrote the passage about attending a Lunt play to include what is obviously a description of "I Know My Love," which did not open on Broadway until the fall of 1949. Thus the only two specific shows mentioned in *The Catcher in the Rye* cannot be used to date the action of the story since they were presented in New York City seven years apart.

Although some of the wittiest lines in *The Catcher in the Rye* are salvaged from "I'm Crazy" and "Slight Rebellion Off Madison," there are large differences between the earlier stories and the novel. Much that happens in *The Catcher in the Rye* between Holden's quarrel with Sally at the ice-skating rink and his later phone call to her is missing from "Slight Rebellion Off Madison"; the long interview with the blasé Carl Luce is described in a paragraph. The story also suffers from being told in the third person about a "mixed-up kid" who is simply on vacation from his school.

Holden's expulsion provides the center of interest, however, in "I'm Crazy," which is told in the first person and contains material later used in *The Catcher in the Rye*—during Holden's opening interview with his history teacher and in the scene in

Phoebe's bedroom. Although it is heresy to say so, I find the short story more realistic than the novel. The Holden of "I'm Crazy" is a vastly different boy from the narrator of *The Catcher in the Rye*. When Phoebe makes the famous remark about Holden's not liking anything that leads, in the novel, to the speech about his being a "catcher in the rye," he replies in the short story simply with a comment about liking the girl he hasn't met yet who sits a few seats ahead of him on the train. He ends up not in a sanitarium but with an office job that he knows he isn't going to like any better than the school from which he has been dismissed. He knows that he just isn't "going to be one of these successful guys."

This early Holden is a much less complex and more familiar type than the boy in the novel—the kind of lazy, romantic kid who loses his keys and breaks his radio and whose intellectual capacities simply do not measure up to his ambitious parents' expectations. He is a boy whom we have all met many times in a society where aspirations often outrun abilities, and his story is affectionately but unsentimentally told. While the later Holden—who cherishes and ultimately loses his illusion of protecting kids from falling over "some crazy cliff"—is a more complex and touching figure than his callow prototype, he is also more pretentious and unrepresentative—he is youth as it would like to fancy itself rather than as it is. In the final version of *The Catcher in the Rye*, Salinger not only altered Holden's personality, but he dropped from the passages retained from "I'm Crazy," one of his most delightful creations, Viola, an infant sister of Holden's and Phoebe's, who climbs out of her crib to beg "Holdie" to get her some "ovvels" (olives).

Before this vastly altered Holden was reintroduced to the public, however, Salinger had emerged from obscurity and become a respected contributor to the *New Yorker,* whose stories appeared in collections of the best of the year. We must, therefore, defer further consideration of Salinger's most famous character until we have examined not only a generally neglected but significant novelette that appeared in *Cosmopolitan* in 1947 but also the group of distinguished short stories that first won Salinger critical recognition.

CHAPTER 5

You, T. S. Eliot

THE LONGEST WORK published by America's most talked about contemporary author during the first decade of his literary career has been almost totally ignored. Only Paul Levine has given "The Inverted Forest" (*Cosmopolitan,* December, 1947) attention anything like proportionate to its bulk. Critics like Gwynn and Blotner have mentioned it only to attack it. They have been largely justified by the awkward form of the story and the obscurity of its purpose; but, like many unsung works, this novelette provides important evidence about some of the persistent assumptions underlying its author's creations.

"The Inverted Forest" deserves attention, for one thing, as a practically unknown slick writer's impudent challenge to the reigning king of literature's Nemi Wood, T. S. Eliot. Eliot, of course, has often been challenged, but rarely by people who have themselves become such respected authors as Salinger. Yet this challenge has gone largely unnoticed since—like the poems the principal figure in "The Inverted Forest" writes—the story "happens to be cerebral enough to require the reader's co-operation." In terms of artistic satisfaction, this cooperation is not repaid; but, if we follow the theory expounded in the story, the reader's needs do not matter anyway. The story proves, upon close examination, to be an allegorical statement of the idea that the artist does not have any social obligations.

The two-part story is—for reasons most critics have considered obscure—narrated by Robert Waner, an employee of a news magazine and an admirer of a woman named Corinne von Nordhoffen, the daughter of a German baron and an heiress to an orthopedic appliances fortune. Corinne "does not lie" and does not like "to be touched unnecessarily." The first pages of the story describe the eleventh birthday of this finicky but tenderhearted rich girl. She has invited a school chum named Raymond Ford, whom she loves because he has avenged an insult she has received; but this knight-errant (who later proves to hail—like Eloise in "Uncle Wiggily in Connecticut"—from that fount of Western innocence, Boise, Idaho) fails to appear. His incredibly vulgar and violent mother, it turns out, has been locked out of her job as a waitress at the local Lobster Palace and has stormed out of town. Raymond disappears from Corinne's life in the wake of this imaginative parent (she relates an obvious fantasy about her high-class origins), who embarrasses and beats him.

The remaining eighty-five per cent of the story concerns Corinne and Raymond's reunion nineteen years later and their ill-fated marriage. The only other man who has attracted Corinne during this period was killed when he fell off the running board of her car. She rediscovers Ford when long-suffering Robert Waner gives her a volume of the other man's poems as a birthday present, along with a note modestly describing Ford as "Coleridge and Blake and Rilke all in one, and more." Actually Ford proves to be an instructor at Columbia. During a rendezvous in a Chinese restaurant, Corinne learns that Ford taught himself to appreciate poetry at the home of a Mrs. Rizzio in Tallahassee, Florida. After quitting his job as a dogtrack tout and ruining his eyes reading twenty-four hours a day at his benefactress' house, Ford went to college and for seven-and-a-half years had nothing in his life "except poetry." He has not even learned to drink and smoke, for he cannot "get past . . . childhood dogmas."

In the course of one of those phone calls that are so numerous and important in Salinger's work, Robert Waner warns Corinne that Ford does not love her; but Corinne, who is still "making private trips back to her childhood," refuses to listen. She marries Ford shortly after the appearance of his second book of poems, *Man on a Carousel*. Ford's first book, *The Cowardly Morning*, incidentally, has attracted so much attention that three people are writing books about it. Ford's reasons for marrying are never explained, but there is no reason to question Waner's theory that Ford "won't be able to think of any reason why he shouldn't."

Shortly after the wedding, a woman calling herself Mary Gates Croft sends Ford an envelope full of poems and then appears on the scene herself. Corinne prevails upon the reluctant

Ford to criticize the manuscripts. One of the most important conversations about the nature of the artist in any of Salinger's works follows. Ford tells the woman whom he supposes to be a young collegian:

> "I can't tell you you're a poet. Because you're not. . . . But you're inventive. . . . A poet doesn't invent his poetry—he finds it. . . . The place . . . where Alph, the sacred river, ran—was found out, not invented. . . . I can't stand any kind of inventiveness."[1]

Despite this devastating judgment which equates "invention" with "phoniness," "Miss" Croft brazenly hangs around and finally—using undisclosed tactics—steals Ford from Corinne. The naïve wife has not the slightest idea that anything is amiss until Ford telephones from the railroad station to tell her that he is leaving New York with the girl, who insists on being called Bunny. He offers no explanation of his behavior and says only that he is sorry. Later Corinne entertains Howie Croft, who turns out to be Bunny's husband, and learns that all of the stories the Croft woman has told are "inventions."

Eighteen months later Ford and Bunny are located in a cheap apartment in a smoky Midwestern city. Ford, who has given up his thick glasses, is taking eye exercises because Bunny thinks he looks like a movie star without his glasses. He obviously sees only with difficulty and he has overcome his childish dogmas enough to have begun to drink heavily. Bunny does not like his work and criticizes him for not writing for money. When Corinne asks Ford to return to New York with her, however, he replies only that he can't get away because he's "with the Brain again." Pressed for an explanation, he replies impatiently with a reference to his vanished mother: "The Brain, the Brain. . . . *You* saw the original. Think back. Think of somebody pounding on the window of a restaurant on a dark street. *You* know the one I mean."[2] Corinne has lost Raymond for a second time because her generous nature is no match for the other woman's violent, underhanded tactics.

Critics have failed to make much of this story. Ihab Hassan discusses it as an example of complete "Oedipal surrender" and argues that "what Thomas Mann presented, in *Tonio Kröger,* as the metaphysical attraction of health and normality for the artist is here rendered as the pathological submission of the outsider to the vulgarian."[3] Paul Levine classifies Ford as "an innocent and talented poet," whose "ascetic childhood left him unequipped to cope with the hard insensitive world in which he must live." Levine also sees Corinne as an outcast "doomed to tragedy," who needs both Ford and society, while Bunny is a symbol of "the corrupt, materialistic loveless world of the grown-up where adult and adultery are synonymous."[4] Gwynn and Blotner in *The Fiction of J. D. Salinger* conclude a summary of the "irredeemably fantastic" plot by asking "and what *is* significant about what *has* happened?"[5] Their further question, "Does all this happen?" is actually more to the point, although they do not pursue it. Hassan's explanation is the most perceptive, but it fails to account for many of the events and the curious, indirect method of narration. The trouble with all of these interpretations is that the critics have been influenced by *The Catcher in the Rye* to consider Salinger as a "realist" and have thus tried to treat the story as much more lifelike than it is. To try to make literal sense of it is to manifest exactly the same characteristics as the doting but unimaginative Corinne in the story.

As psychologically realistic fiction, "The Inverted Forest" is surely one of the least satisfactory tales ever written, but it can be justified as an allegory. That an allegory is intended is suggested by the only lines of Ford's poetry actually quoted in the story, "Not wasteland, but a great inverted forest / with all foliage underground," from which the title of the story is taken. Since we are also told that during his days in Florida, Ford read a little Eliot, the "wasteland" referred to in the poem must surely be the twentieth-century West as emblemized by Eliot. Ford's poem answers Eliot by asserting that the world is not really all wasteland, all "phony," but that the "nice" world exists beneath the surface (in the mind) where beautiful, green things grow that cannot be observed externally. Salinger actually uses the term "underground" in this passage in a manner remarkably similar to that of the "disaffiliated" writers of the Beat Generation. The apartment Ford shares with Bunny also foreshadows the Beatnik "pad." Although Salinger speaks slightingly of the Beats in the opening section of "Seymour: An Introduction," he is distinguished from them only because he clings to certain upper-middle-class notions about avoiding conspicuous dress and indecorous public behavior. The labels *Beatsville* and

Squaresville can be applied without much stretching to Salinger's "nice" and "phony" worlds, respectively.

Since, according to Ford's poem, what beauties the world possesses are all "underground," one need not be able to "see" them in any material sense. One can live entirely within his imagination. The title of Ford's second book of poems, *Man on a Carousel,* which recalls Holden Caulfield's delight near the end of *The Catcher in the Rye* at the sight of Phoebe riding around and around on the carousel, is a further indication of the poet's rejection of the busy world of news magazines and cocktail parties where people are constantly preoccupied with "getting somewhere."

The concept expressed in Ford's poem evidently evolved as a result of the experiences described in the story. He spent his childhood in the "wasteland," but he found a certain security there since he knew no other world. (Salinger is less concerned about the particular kind of atmosphere in which a child grows up than he is about the wrench when the child leaves his familiar world for any other.) Through Mrs. Rizzio, Ford discovers the "nice" world of poetry, which is "underground" in the sense that it is concealed within books (Salinger may not have deliberately intended "foliage" in the lines of poetry quoted to refer to the "leaves" of books, but the possible play on words strengthens the image), but he practically loses his sight while discovering it. The glasses which enable Ford to see the real world again and the enthusiastic reception of his books encourage him temporarily to leave the comfortable world of his imagination for Corinne's luxurious world; but he has never been trained to get along in society (his remark that "he don't mix too well with people" is classic understatment). Because he cannot get past "childhood dogmas," he is ill-at-ease among the sophisticates who seek his advice, and Corinne cannot help him because she is still trying to recapture her own childhood.

The day that Corinne first insists he meet Bunny Croft and then entertains some unexpected, intoxicated callers until midnight, Ford learns that life with his wife will oblige him to sacrifice his work to time-wasting visitors. Living with the jealous Bunny, who is unwilling to share him, enables him, on the other hand, to retreat back into the world of his imagination, to seek escape from the real world by removing his glasses and by drinking. Robert Waner is, in short, entirely right when he says that Ford is "the most gigantic psychotic you'll ever know" if by "psychotic" he means a person who withdraws from the "wasteland" of society to dwell exclusively in the "inverted forest" of his imagination.

But why does Ford call Bunny (and his mother), the "Brain"? Why does he run off with a woman whom he criticizes violently and who does not like his work? Is this—as Levine implies—a tale of adultery, or—as Hassan suggests—a tragedy of mother-fixation? I think it is neither. Waner, the narrator, tries to warn Corinne that Ford does not—cannot—love her, because "a man just can't reach the kind of poetry Ford's reaching and still keep intact the normal male ability to spot a fine hat-straightener." As Waner also sees in one of Ford's expressions, the poet "suspects himself of having, at some time in his life, either lost or forfeited some natural interior dimension of mysterious importance."[6] This "dimension" is the ability to reciprocate another's affection. Ford must live entirely within the world of his imagination, which he can share with others only through his writings.

The only thing he needs another person for is to protect him against intruders—a "brain" to solve the problems of providing for him physically. Corinne has made the fatal mistake of expecting Ford to do things both for her and for other people; she and Ford are hopelessly mismated because both are looking for a kind of help and protection that the other cannot provide. Corinne is at the same time too painfully honest and literal minded to share Ford's world of the imagination; Bunny, on the other hand, is completely "phony"; but, like Ford's mother, she "invents" the very kind of physical punishments and "wasteland" art that tortures the sensitive soul of the poet and forces him to escape back into the world of his imagination. Bunny is not, however, a "mother" in the emotional sense, but the kind of "keeper" that his real mother was. The "silver cord" in this story is a chain. Rarely has the idea that the creation of art demands that the artist suffer personally ever been more appallingly allegorized.

There are thus no reasons to suppose that there is any sexual motive for Ford's flight with Bunny. Ford is one of the many Salinger characters who show no interest in sex at all. He regards Bunny with awe only as a "brain," and not at all as a body. While the story—as Ihab Hassan points out—surely involves an "Oedipal surrender," the surrender has no erotic overtones. Ford simply wishes to remain a child and to have his mother—or the figure who replaces her—shield him from *all* responsibilities. Ford's wife Corinne cooked her own goose when she demanded that Ford act maturely by taking a kind of paternal interest in Bunny. If Corinne had wished to keep him, she should have built a wall around him and fiercely fended off all interlopers.

The reader misses the point of the story, in fact, if he agrees with Corinne, when she at last finds Ford in his Midwestern hideout, that "everything was wrong with him." What is "wrong" from the viewpoint of Corinne's success-oriented world may be "right" from the viewpoint of the artist who doesn't want to get anywhere anyway, but wants only to dwell in the "inverted forest" of his imagination. What the normal "thinking" man considers "wrong" may not, as Robert Waner points out, matter to the artist anyway; for—according to the aesthetic principle that Ford announces during his first conversation with Bunny— a writer does not "invent" poetry, employing the formulas that society provides, but "finds" it in the mysterious depths of his imagination.

This concept of art as something "found" rather than "invented" underlies all of Salinger's work, and it partly explains why he sympathizes with those who learn through blinding revelations (like Lois Taggett and Eloise and Holden Caulfield and De Daumier-Smith) rather than through methodical thinking. Certainly if "The Inverted Forest" is read as an allegory of the plight of the imaginative artist in the modern, mechanistic, success-oriented world, most of the objections that have been made to it can be countered.

Robert Waner must serve as the narrator, for example, because he is the only character who can supply the necessary interpretations of Ford's motives: he can both admire him as a poet (which Bunny can't) and dislike him as a social creature (which Corinne can't). The reasons behind many of the events in the story are not explained because the explanations are not relevant to the allegory. All that is essential in the story is that which elucidates the artist's relationship to his work and to other members of society.

This view involves quarreling with Eliot not only because

Eliot's poetry—since it is largely based upon traditional learn-ing—is "invented" rather than "found," but also because Eliot—like Corinne—wishes to reform the wasteland rather than to withdraw into "the inverted forest." Waner verbalizes Ford's basic assumption about art when he insists to Corinne that "poets"—as opposed to versifiers—don't really understand other people's feelings at all, but write "under pressure of dead-weight beauty." Apparently this is the same pressure that Ford suggests drove Corinne's mother to commit suicide. "Dead weight beauty" can only mean a burden so heavy that the true artist cannot choose but to be completely irresponsible socially. Corinne, however, cannot even conceive of an activity that does not involve understanding and "helping" other people.

Although the story can be defended against earlier criticisms if it is viewed as an allegorical presentation of a doctrine that exempts the artist from all social responsibility, it has serious shortcomings. The first is that the theory that the pursuit of one's artistic vision justifies ignoring all one's obligations to society is the most self-indulgent kind of sentimentality—identical with the Beatnik notion of "disaffiliation." Salinger, however—like many of his characters—evades stating the position directly, since he probably wishes to avoid the conspicuous flaunting of respectability that causes many people (including Salinger in "Seymour: An Introduction") to spurn the exhibitionistic Beats. Instead he expresses his concept of "disaffiliation" obscurely in the kind of middle-class magazine whose readers would prob-ably not even recognize, let alone accept, the idea. By publish-ing the story in such a magazine, Salinger is able both to insult its conventional readers without their realizing it and to avoid the risk of being read by those distastefully unconventional persons who might embarrass him by proclaiming that they shared his views.

To embody his sentimental notions, furthermore, Salinger had to create characters that were overdrawn even for an allegory. All are unnaturally handsome. The reception of Ford's poetry is incredible; not even Eliot or Salinger himself has received the kind of adulation described in this story. Corinne is too naïve and candid to be a convincing representative of the slick world of Wellesley and the news magazines. Bunny is too gifted at inventing appealing tales to live very long in squalor or to need to tie herself down to Raymond Ford any more than to Howie Croft. (The story is obviously written from the viewpoint of a man with little respect for feminine pride and discretion.) The criticism of Eliot is likely to please only those who are willing to accept squalor as the price of irresponsibility. The story, in short—and perhaps this is the only criticism that needs to be made of it—appears to have been "invented" rather than "found."

CHAPTER 6

The Desired Effect

W ITH "A Perfect Day for Bananafish" we emerge from the thicket of yellowing magazine leaves into the much frequented clearing of *Nine Stories,* where critics have often performed their rituals. The first story to win Salinger a prominent place in the *New Yorker* ("Slight Rebellion Off Madison," when it finally did appear, was an "extra" story hidden back among the chic advertisements), "Bananafish" was also one of the fifty-five stories to be included in an anthology of those published in the magazine during the 1940's. It has since been the subject of more comment than possibly any other short story of its period, largely because it introduces to the reading public the fabulous Seymour Glass.

Before considering this famous story, however, we must glance briefly at the single new short story that Salinger had printed between the Babe Gladwaller-Holden Caulfield tales of 1945 and the preface to the Glass legend. "A Young Girl in 1941 with No Waist at All" is his sole contribution to date to the fashionable *Mademoiselle,* which has sandwiched the works of many distinguished writers between its fashion plates. The story—for whose Caribbean cruise-ship background Salinger may have ransacked his own past[1]—is especially interesting as a turgid and ambiguous exploration of the ideas that were to jell in "Uncle Wiggily in Connecticut," for "A Young Girl . . ." also deals with "the last minutes" of girlhood—those that the dejected Eloise, in the more famous story, had spent with the whimsical Walt.

In "A Young Girl . . . ," the title character is a self-effacing orphan who has been "sick" and is now cruising the Caribbean with her mother-in-law-to-be. The girl, Barbara, is apparently drifting into marriage because—not having gone to college—she cannot think of anything else to do (like Salinger's earlier character Lois Taggett and James Purdy's Malcolm). Her acquaintances have apparently convinced her that she is stupid and awkward, and when Ray Kinsella, tall member of the ship's entertainment committee, asks her what her fiancé is like she can only say that "he sounds lovely over the telephone" and "he is very—very considerate about stuff." She admits that she can never understand what boys are talking about. After Kinsella demonstrates a romantic interest in her (as usual in a Salinger story, they do no more than kiss), she returns to her stateroom and tells her traveling companion that she does not wish to get married at all, which is—Barbara supposes—just what her fiancé's mother wishes to hear. Apparently when Barbara makes a decision on her own, she leaves her girlhood behind.

The story might have been a slight but effective revelation of a young woman's awakening consciousness of her responsibility for herself if Salinger had not introduced two other motifs that he never really succeeds in relating to Barbara's transformation. A "stinking rich" Mr. and Mrs. Woodruff provide an example of what marriage should be. Although Mrs. Woodruff points out that by this time they should have drifted apart, their marriage remains a joy to them in their middle age. How they might serve as an example to the perplexed Barbara, however, is obscure, since neither she nor anyone else overhears the conversation that reveals their significance as a symbol of continued marital bliss. There is also much talk—largely from the Woodruffs—about the tragic conditions in 1941 with young men being called into the service, young girls being left alone at home, and cruise ships being converted into troop ships; but it is never demonstrated that any of these admittedly unhappy occurrences has any direct bearing on Barbara's decision.

What suddenly enabled the author of this and a dozen-and-a-half other uncelebrated stories to contribute to the January 31, 1948, issue of the *New Yorker* five pages consisting almost entirely of dialogue that were to become one of the most frequently discussed short stories of the postwar period? Salinger isn't talking, nor are those on the magazine's staff who might know; but I can't help wondering how much of the unprecedented effectiveness of "A Perfect Day for Bananafish" may be attributed to the magazine's rigorous editorial work. The trouble with many of Salinger's earlier stories had been that they lacked a single, clear focus; their effects were dissipated by extraneous background material.

While nothing has ever been said publicly about editing Salinger's manuscripts, another distinguished writer has told me that one of his stories was drastically altered and cut to about half its original length by the *New Yorker* editors. A comparison of the book and magazine versions of a long work like Elizabeth Spencer's *Light in the Piazza* also illustrates the detailed revisions the magazine may make in even a major work by an established author. Certainly judicious pruning would have immensely benefited "The Inverted Forest" and "A Young Girl. . . ."

Whatever happened, "A Perfect Day for Bananafish" as finally published has—like "Uncle Wiggily in Connecticut"—the tight three-act structure of a well-made play. So theatrical, in fact, is the story that is seems to challenge an imaginative director and designer to devise an expressionistic treatment of it to set off the fanciful second act from the startlingly realistic first and third. Perhaps the author—who had long been interested in dramatics and the movies—wrote with a vision of how a motion picture could even better achieve the desired effect.

Certainly the dramatic possibilities are made evident by an outline of the story. In the first "act," the young wife of a mentally disturbed war veteran reports in the course of a telephone conversation with her mother in New York that, during an automobile trip to Miami Beach, the husband made some conscious progress in efforts to gain control of himself. She stresses that he avoided looking at trees (apparently he had earlier driven a car into a tree.)[2] The reader can even imagine the strident voice of the unseen mother filling the stage or screen as the girl holds the telephone receiver at increasing angles from her ear.

In the second "act," the husband, whom even the hotel psychiatrist has recognized as "sick," is shown on the beach gently and admirably admonishing a very small girl against being jealous of other small girls and mistreating animals. At the same time he excites her imagination with a tale of fantastic bananafish who die after they are trapped by their gluttony. The rapidly moving third "act" is divided into two scenes. In the first, in a hotel elevator, Seymour Glass, the man whom we met on the beach, accuses a woman he does not know, of staring at his feet, just as his wife has reported he has earlier accused people of starting at a nonexistent tattoo. In the second scene, he extracts an automatic revolver from his luggage in the hotel room, lies down on the unoccupied twin bed, looks significantly at his sleeping wife in the other bed, and fires "a bullet through his right temple."

Previous critics have followed two lines about this story of a suicide. Some—misled I believe by the deadpan dramatic structure of the story—describe it as simply a collection of fragmentary scenes transcribing with clinical accuracy the events of the day on which a psychotic finally succeeds in killing himself. Others, who have taken the disturbed Seymour's description of his wife as "Miss Spiritual Tramp of 1948" at face value, have read into Seymour's story of the bananafish a pathetic metaphorical account of his own entrapment and have considered the story (as Gwynn and Blotner do) as an allegory of the fate of a hypersensitive man in a materialistic and meretricious world—Salinger's "phony" world. Both interpretations help explain the story, but they cannot be reconciled with each other, since it is impossible to accept Seymour's evaluations of situations if he is really psychotic. If, on the other hand, he is the only sane man in a world gone mad, there should be no quibbling over the sanity of his committing suicide. So hypnotic is the effect of Salinger's style that no small part of the success of the story is attributable to the reader's becoming inclined to accept Seymour's statement without quibble. Yet we should be slow to endorse an irrationally motivated suicide.

If we ponder the title that Seymour bestows upon his wife, we may begin to question whether it is really applicable. While it is hard to tell just what the distraught young man means by "spiritual tramp," the term carefully implies someone who has no fixed convictions or stable set of values, whose *modus operandi* is pure expediency. Muriel, Seymour's wife, hardly deserves this title. Her defects are that she is gossipy, overly concerned about trivial material things, and—principally—that she neglects great works of the imagination like Rilke's poetry. (Even if Rilke were not praised elsewhere in Salinger's work, his imagination and sensitivity make it obvious that to Seymour he would be the "only great poet of the century," whom he wishes Muriel to read in German.)

She is not, however, unstable or without the courage of her

convictions. From her telephone conversation, we learn that she has waited through the war for Seymour, has waited again for his release from a military hospital, has allowed him to drive against her parent's wishes, and is willing to defend vigorously both herself and Seymour from her parents' meddling. As Ihab Hassan points out in *Radical Innocence,* Muriel's mother is certainly one of the most vicious busybodies in literature, but Muriel isn't. Far from being upset by circumstances, in fact, Muriel is a tower of coolly self-controlled strength, as is apparent from the author's initial description of her as "a girl who for a ringing phone dropped exactly nothing." Such composure is actually quite a rare mark of tough-mindedness in a neurotic society that jumps when bells ring and horns honk.

It is precisely this kind of composure, however, that would annoy, even more than the jangling noises, the psychotic who is overwhelmed by the insistent demands a fast-moving society makes upon him. Such a disturbed person would not admire composure; he would resent it because it accentuated his own maladjustment. The disturbed individual might quite inappropriately describe the undisturbed person as "a spiritual tramp" in an effort to disrupt the other's composure.

In "A Perfect Day for Bananafish," Seymour does many things —intentionally or unintentionally—to disrupt others' composure. How would most people react to being accused of staring at a non-existent tattoo? How would people react to a man so disrespectful of age and femininity as to ask a grandmother about her plans for passing away?—to a man so disrespectful of "beauty" as to do something unmentionable to "lovely pictures from Bermuda"? What kind of person plays the piano every night in the public rooms of a resort hotel that attracts a convention of advertising men? Certainly a person who actually drove into a tree or even threatened to drive into one would disrupt others' composure and attract attention to himself.

Seymour disconcerts a number of people in the story. He disrupts Sybil Carpenter's haughty juvenile composure several times. He describes her bathing suit as blue (which his is), and he makes her emphatically point out twice that it is really yellow. When they enter the water, he keeps pushing her out to sea on the float, until she is obliged to tell him not to go too far. Even though she has not had enough of skipping waves on the float, she must return to shore at his whim immediately after she acknowledges that she has seen one of the fantastic bananafish he has described. Even his kissing the arch of her foot is not only a gesture of humble gratitude, but also an action that makes her turn around, flustered. Although the parentally neglected Sybil learns some useful lessons about tolerance from Seymour, she also provides him with great ego-satisfaction.

So does the inoffensive woman on the elevator. When Seymour accuses her of staring at his feet, her composure is so ruffled that she demands to be let off. She has paid attention to him. But Muriel has not. She has been patient and understanding, but she has not read Rilke when told. She has even regarded Seymour's driving the car into a tree as part of his "condition" and has insisted upon his therapeutically driving again. What effect is this tactful firmness likely to have upon a person like Seymour who is happiest in the company of small children?

Everyone is familiar with the kind of small children who demand that adults—and playmates, too—pay constant attention to them. If they do not attract the attention they crave or if old methods fail to provoke the desired effects, they devise constantly more conspicuous and dangerous things to win the coveted notice. Shouting, "Daddy, look at me now," they climb farther and farther up the tree, run faster without watching where they are going, perform more desperate tricks, show how long they can hold onto the lit firecracker. The most aggressive may actually harm others, but more often these juvenile exhibitionists inflict injury upon themselves. Ignoring them does not make them stop; it only makes them behave more hysterically.

Seymour is so much at ease with Sybil and so uneasy with adults because—as his uncontrollable desire to be the center of attention shows—he is still childish. He is not childlike, which would mean he retained the child's spontaneity while being responsible for his actions, but he is downright childish. He has retained children's most petulant characteristics, not their most engaging. His childishness has enabled him to disconcert many stuffy adults, but Muriel's tough, understanding composure remains unruffled. He has not gotten her to do what he wishes—particularly to read Rilke. She even "trusts" him to take care of himself on the beach while she phones her mother. He has tried in increasingly conspicuous ways to upset her, even by driving the car into a tree. Finally, as with the child so desperate for the desired attention that it will risk injury, there remains but one thing he can do—he can shoot himself. Then she will have to pay attention; then her iron composure will be disrupted. She will cry and run hysterically about the hotel room—or so he hopes.

I suspect that really Muriel's composure would not be disrupted, for she seems to be the kind of imperturbable fortress that survives even the most violent blow. If she were not discomposed, Seymour's suicide would be a double tragedy, for he would have died without achieving the desired effect. But speculation about her behavior lie outside this story, which is Seymour's, not Muriel's.

We cannot know whether Seymour's desperate behavior is deliberate or not, but I suspect that it is *not*, since his actions seem impulsive rather than carefully planned. Part of this trouble seems to be anguish over his physical maturing, which has partly isolated him from Sybil's world. Whether Seymour's actions are preconceived or impulsive, his suicide is a demented act. Paul Levine come close to the truth about Seymour's suicide when he says that it is caused by the character's "inability to communicate"; but Levine does not go on to consider what Seymour wishes to communicate—especially his enthusiasm for Rilke and for giving free rein to one's imagination. Although he may not be able to articulate his grievances, Seymour is definitely not a "rebel without a cause." He believes that the world of well-composed people which Muriel represents has lost the child-like exuberance that reading Rilke and romancing about bananafish might restore. His feelings have been intensified by Sybil's response to his fantasies, so that he returns to his room in the tensest possible state of excitement. His suicide is not at all, as Ihab Hassan suggests, "a cleansing act." It is rather like the final excesses of Kafka's "Hunger Artist"—the last desperate resource of the would-be publicist of an ignored cause.

Thus, despite its dramatic structure, "A Perfect Day for Bananafish" is not best read as the kind of progressive narrative in which the meaning of all that happens up to any given point is clear without considering the whole. Rather it needs to be read as a kind of extended metaphor in which every detail contributes to the complete structure and must be interpreted in relation to the whole. It is a narrative of the principal events of the day on which a paranoid commits suicide; but the reasons for his killing himself are not unfathomable—they are implicit in the events described.

It is also the story of a man who fancies himself trapped like a sated bananafish; but we must recall that this is a man who is not trapped by an external situation beyond his control—like Eloise in "Uncle Wiggily in Connecticut"—but by an internal sickness. Readers who consider Seymour a victim of society are as sick as Seymour himself. Wiegand points out that there is "no demonstrated connection between society's insensitivity and Seymour's zaniness."[3] This statement is true if it means that Seymour has not—like the Joads in *The Grapes of Wrath*, for example, and other characters in "social protest" fiction—been denied the basic external requirements to maintain human dignity; but it is not true if it means that he has not been denied the extraordinary attention he craves. Even in his pathetic tale about the bananafish, Seymour recognizes that he has been trapped by some impulse within himself and not by snares laid by others. He is actually a character like Tularecito in Steinbeck's *The Pastures of Heaven*—a gifted young man who cannot restrain his violent impulses enough to enable him to live in society. The fact that Seymour has a fleeting insight into his condition, which Tularecito is denied, makes his situation even more poignant. He is the glutton that he describes the bananafish as being; but his insatiable appetite is for attention.

Just what Salinger felt should have been done about the situation he describes is not clear, nor is it relevant, since he is an artist, not a social reformer. He appears outraged by the destruction of someone with Seymour's sensitivity, yet resigned to it—as to Joe Varioni's and to Raymond Ford's in "The Inverted Forest." He shows that Seymour has been mishandled, but he does not suggest how he could have been better handled or even if better handling were possible.

I think it is a mistake to read material from the later works about Seymour Glass into his early story, as William Wiegand does, for example, when he says that "the story needs the background of the later Glass family narratives to give Seymour's suicide its full reference." Over the years the character has obviously developed in Salinger's mind; and when we consider "A Perfect Day for Bananafish" in isolation from the later stories we realize that the original Seymour was not at all "surfeited," but rather that he demanded more of others than they were capable of providing.

The one thing that can be said about the relationship of the author's career to "A Perfect Day for Bananafish" is that this pathetic story of a man whose pathological need to have an effect upon other people finally drove him to suicide enabled Salinger at last to attract the attention of the public and to break into the ranks of the regular contributors to one of the nation's most influential magazines. The "perfect day" was the death of Seymour Glass, but the making of J. D. Salinger, who, ironically, was within a few years to find himself trapped by his own fame.

About the same time that "A Perfect Day for Bananafish" appeared, *Good Housekeeping* gave its seal of approval to "A Girl I Knew," which deals unsuccessfully with the same problem of the world's insensitivity to the destruction of innocence. The charming Viennese Jewess, Leah, is, however, genuinely childlike; whereas Seymour is childish. Instead of killing herself, she suffers the awful fate of dying in a Nazi concentration camp after having been forced by her parents to marry a man she scarcely knows.

Gwynn and Blotner complain about the inappropriateness of "the parody style" of the first part of this story (in which the young American narrator talks German to Leah, while she speaks to him in English) to an account of a victim of the Hitler regime; but the real trouble is that the early whimsy is entirely appropriate, since Leah is a frail and wispish character who appears doomed to have her fragile and timorous personality suppressed whether the Nazis destroy her or not. The story is not really effective as a protest against the inhumanity of the Nazis because their victim is a girl who would surely have been defeated by external forces anyway. As in "A Young Girl in 1941 with No Waist at All," Salinger does not really succeed in establishing any connection between the background of his story and the characters in the foreground.

Actually Salinger's purpose in "A Girl I Knew" seems to be not so much to stimulate pity for Leah and hatred toward the Nazis as to arouse antipathy for those Americans who are unmoved by the knowledge of her destruction. As in "Soft Boiled Sergeant," a human tragedy becomes simply the vehicle for distinguishing the "nice" people from the "phonies." At the end of the story, the narrator returns to the apartment house where he and Leah's family had resided only to find it converted into quarters for American officers. He is almost frustrated in his sentimental journey by a boorish non-commissioned officer in charge of the quarters, who is so busy catering to the officers that he fails to be moved by the revelation of Leah's unhappy fate (it is even hinted that he is anti-Semitic). While the reader is outraged by this man's indifference to human bestiality, he is also left with the uncomfortable impression that sympathy has been enlisted .for the simple and gentle Leah only to emphasize the coldbloodedness of the chargé of quarters. Gwynn and Blotner are correct when they assert that the matter of this story is "too deep for tears." Salinger has far less success dealing with a genuinely childlike person like Leah than with the childish Seymour, because those who are destroyed by others' inhumanity deserve far more deferential treatment than those who court disaster. Salinger's whole artistic approach is too flippant to do justice to truly pathetic cases. A writer who sentimentally exploits helpless victims of Nazi depravity is guilty of tastelessness, but he is surely less guilty than those who chose "A Girl I Knew" over "A Perfect Day for Bananafish" and "Uncle Wiggily in Connecticut" as a "prize story" of the year.

"A Young Girl in 1941 with No Waist at All," "A Perfect Day for Bananafish," and "A Girl I Knew" are all unbalanced portrayals of the destruction of childlike innocence. Not until Salinger was able to create a character strong and self-conscious enough to recognize and, in some fashion, to adjust to drab reality was he able to draw clearly the line separating the "nice" from the "phony" world. A month after Seymour Glass's debut in "A Perfect Day for Bananafish," this character was to appear in "Uncle Wiggily in Connecticut," which—as we have already seen—provides a key to Salinger's view of man and his disconcerting universe.

CHAPTER 7

A Grand Bunch of Kids

AFTER having successfully dramatized a vision that had haunted him from the beginning of his career, an artist might be satisfied simply to sit back and work out variations on the successful story. Salinger, however, has always been restless; and once he had succeeded, in "Uncle Wiggily in Connecticut," in depicting the difference between the "nice" and "phony" worlds as he discerned them, he became absorbed with what had been a subordinate consideration in "A Perfect Day for Bananafish" and "Uncle Wiggily"—the reaction of a child or adolescent to the disillusioning discovery of the phoniness of the adult world. This absorption was to culminate in Holden Caulfield's recognition, in the final version of *The Catcher in the Rye,* that children can't be kept from grabbing for the gold ring.

I *"Just Before the War with the Eskimos"*

As might be expected when an artist begins to wrestle with a new problem, the earlier stories of the new group fail to measure up to the artistic standard set by "Uncle Wiggily in Connecticut." Although the first, "Just Before the War with the Eskimos," bears one of Salinger's most imaginative titles, it suffers from mechanical plotting and from the imposition on the basic story of obvious symbolism uncharacteristic of Salinger's work. James E. Bryan in "J. D. Salinger: The Fat Lady and the Chicken Sandwich" (*College English,* December, 1961) ingeniously finds Christian symbolism in many of the details of the story; but his reading tends to obscure the quite realistic problem in human relations that the story presents.

As Gwynn and Blotner point out, "Eskimos" is the story of teen-age Ginnie's abrogation of her demand to be reimbursed for taxi fares after she visits the apartment of a tennis-ball manufacturer and discovers the "pathetic situation" of her schoolmate Selena's "24-year-old misfit brother" Franklin. Some details of the critics' analysis, however, need amplification. The text strongly implies that Franklin's friend Eric is not just "effeminate" but homosexual. In reply to a question about whether he spent the war working in an aircraft factory because of a bad heart, he replies, "Heavens, no . . . I have the constitution of . . . ." After this comment is interrupted, Ginnie refuses—for unexplained reasons—to speak to him again. Eric's difficulties with a once much-pampered male "writer" who has run out on his host, Eric's 4-F status, and Ginnie's sudden coolness are all difficult to explain unless the man is actually perverted; for homosexuality is one subject that excites great confusion and bitter resentment the few times it is even hinted at in Salinger's writings.

It is also especially ironic that Ginnie's sister, who has snubbed the "misfit" brother whose heart disqualified him for military service, is going to marry a naval officer—something the brother could never aspire to be. The irony of his situation also gives double meaning to his outburst about "the war with the Eskimos," which gives the story its title. His bitter assertion that this time only "the old guys" will go denounces the older generation both because it starts wars that younger men must fight and because it has borne him with a defective heart that has cut him off from the company of his normal contemporaries in the armed forces. His refusal to return to college could be prompted by the knowledge that he would be asked embarrassing questions by the war veterans who in 1948 comprised the majority of student bodies.

The "pathetic situation" that Ginnie discovers is thus the same as that from which Eloise suffers in "Uncle Wiggily in Connecticut"—man is at the mercy of an indifferent and absurd universe in which the blame for tragic accidents (like a defective heart) cannot be satisfactorily assigned. (Salinger's view of the universe resembles that of many of the Existentialists, but he consistently shies away from their philosophy that, in the face of such an "absurd" universe, individuals must accept the responsibility for making their own choices. He may feel that accepting such responsibility would mean forsaking the childish qualities he prizes.) Ginnie's renunciation of the money at the end of the story is her attempt to keep Selena—whom she had previously considered the "biggest drip" at school—from drifting into the same state of pathetic isolation as Franklin, who is compelled to seek out the company of a shrill pervert who considers Franklin's conventional taste in movies "impossible."

If the story had ended with Ginnie's kindly gesture, we might overlook the artificial situation that Salinger is obliged to devise (the story has more "entrances" and "exits" than a French bedroom farce) in order that Ginnie may have interviews alone with both Franklin and Eric. The author supposed it necessary, however, to reinforce his point with some of the sleaziest symbolism to appear in any of his stories. Ginnie is described as a girl who had once kept a dead Easter chick three days in a wastebasket-tomb before disposing of it. She is introduced into a disunified and neurasthenic family: the unseen father is described as doing nothing but providing balls, the mother is bedridden, the son and daughter become nearly hysterical over slight physical and emotional injuries. These embellishments can hardly be accounted for except as part of an allegorical representation of the introduction of Christian compassion into a household obsessed with the most superficial and physical aspects of existence.

While Ginnie's renunciation of the money seems a genuinely thoughtful act, her keeping the uneaten parts of ˜a sandwich Franklin presses upon her seems as maudlinly sentimental as Franklin's swearing exaggeratedly in an effort to assert a virility which his actions deny. By overitalicizing his point almost as badly as his character Eric overitalicizes his remarks, Salinger—instead of stressing the "conversion" that subordinates Ginnie's superficial toughness to her internal kindness—kills with an overdose of allegory his story of the plight of spiritually "good-hearted" people in a world preoccupied with purely physical concerns.

II "*Blue Melody*"

Another not completely successful story of "youth's awakening" appeared a few months later in *Cosmopolitan*. Gwynn and Blotner are wrong when they assert that "Blue Melody" "wants to be about Lisa Jones, a Negro blues singer who (in a situation based on accounts of the tragic end of Bessie Smith) dies from appendicitis because the Southern white hospitals to which she is taken will not admit her."[1] The story is actually about a white boy named Rudford, whose boyhood ends with Lisa's death. The climax of the story is heavily emphasized when the narrator, to whom Rudford has told his story, says that the boy feared his world might end while his eyes were closed at a picnic which he attends with Lisa and other friends, black and white; and, further, that Rudford awakened to find that indeed his world had ended. The "end" is caused, of course, by Lisa's dying after she is stricken during the picnic before he can find a hospital that will admit her.

After Lisa's death, Rudford leaves the South. When, years later during the war, he again meets the white girl who shared these experiences with him and finds her the wife of a jealous army officer who is uninterested in her childhood ordeal, Rudford promises to play one of Lisa's rare recordings for his old companion sometime, but he never does. He does not want to because the record is "terribly scratchy" and Lisa's voice can hardly be recognized. The implication of this seeming rudeness is that recollections of his youth have become effaced and he does not wish to bring them back; he has had to spend his life living down his shame at the "phoniness" of the world, and especially that of the white South.

Salinger stresses at the beginning of the story that despite the criticism of white Southern hospitals, the story "isn't a slam" against any one particular section of the country; it is "just a simple little story of mom's apple pie, ice-cold beer, the Brooklyn Dodgers, and the Lux Theatre of the Air—the things we fought for—in short." These were indeed the things that the more sentimental propagandists of the period said that Americans were fighting for, and this story comes as close as anything that Salinger has written to criticizing the "phony" heroic pose of a country that fights for freedom abroad and still practices fatal discrimination at home.

The story—which also begins with an amusing sideswipe at the "theatrical" military personalities like General George Patton —fails, however, to achieve what appears to be its purpose of dramatizing one boy's awakening to the realities of the American situation. It fails because of the contrast between the sharp sarcasm of the opening passage, part of which I have quoted, and the subtlety of the conclusion. If Salinger really thought as much explanation as he provides at the beginning was necessary, he should have explained more specifically Rudford's feelings at the end of the story. If, on the other hand, the boy's unique awakening to the realities of the "phony" world are to be emphasized, the satirical introduction should have been dropped. In this story, as in "This Sandwich Has No Mayonnaise" and "A Girl I Knew," inconsistencies in tone mar the overall effectiveness of the work.

Also despite Salinger's disclaimer, a story that deals with a talented Negro in western Tennessee being accorded the kind of treatment it describes cannot avoid appearing to be an attack upon the evils of a particular section rather than upon the irresponsibility of the nation as a whole. "Blue Melody" is unimpressive because the individual characters are not memorable enough to permit it to stand beside *The Catcher in the Rye* as an account of one boy's initiation into life; yet the situation is not sufficiently generalized to allow the story to serve as an indictment of national irresponsibility. Probably Salinger erred in choosing to recall the tragic history of a colorful celebrity like Bessie Smith (subsequently used to much greater advantage by Edward Albee in his play *The Death of Bessie Smith*), since the moving account of her fate overshadows the story of Rudford, who should have been the central character if the story were to have a unified impact.

III *"The Laughing Man"*

Salinger must have had special difficulties fashioning a satisfactory tale of "youth's awakening," because half a year elapsed before his next story, "The Laughing Man," was published in the *New Yorker*. It suffered from the same kind of overly complex structure as "Just Before the War with the Eskimos" and "Blue Melody." Also concerned with a child's disillusionment, "The Laughing Man" is poignant enough upon first reading to leave the reader's teeth "chattering uncontrollably" like the young narrator's at end of the story; but the more closely we examine the story, the more questions it provokes.

The problems the story poses are apparent from two different interpretations of it. Ihab Hassan comments in *Radical Innocence* that the tale shows that the story-telling ability of a man frustrated in love is "powerless" to save him; but William Wiegand reads it as a consideration of "sublimation in art" as a possible remedy for the gluttonous inability to distinguish between experiences that threatens to destroy Salinger's "banana-fish" heroes. Wiegand's position appears sounder; but either intepretation can be justified because of Salinger's failure to deal with a crucial question at the end of the story.

As Gywnn and Blotner point out, "The Laughing Man" is "the recollection by a mature man of a crucial experience at the age of nine." The narrator recalls belonging as a boy to a group of "Comanches," which John Gedsudski—a short, ugly, self-made man in his early twenties—supervises to pay his way through school. Gedsudki has progressed from apparently humble origins on Staten Island via the athletic field to the New York University law school, enjoying enormous success at each stage in his progress. Besides teaching his young charges games, Gedsudski entertains them each day with installments of a fantastic story about a remarkably ugly but fantastically wealthy "Laughing Man," who is clearly a projection of the tale-teller himself. (Gwynn and Blotner trace the story to Victor Hugo's L'homme Que Rit, but Salinger could have been drawing upon recollections of his childhood and need not have been aware of Hugo's story.)

Gedsudski is attracted to Mary Hudson, a wealthy Long Island girl who has attended Wellesley. Much to the surprise of the "Comanches," when Mary insists upon joining their baseball game she proves to be an excellent batter. After some time, however, for reasons that the young narrator cannot fathom, Gedsudski and Mary quarrel and she runs off. That night, Gedsudski kills the hero of his episodic tale and the story ends "never to be revived." The youngest "Comanche" breaks into tears and even the more sophisticated narrator is so traumatized that, when he sees a piece of red tissue paper reminiscent of the laughing man's mask flapping about a lamp-post, his teeth begin chattering uncontrollably.[2]

The story at first seems unsatisfactory because the young narrator cannot tell what has happened between Gedsudski and Mary and the reader can think of not too few but of too many possible explanations. Knowing the cause of the lover's quarrel is, however, irrelevant to understanding the story; for it does not concern the romantic break-up, but the effects of this break-up on the impressionable young narrator: he suffers the double disillusionment of seeing the man he idolizes frustrated and of losing a source of innocent pleasure with the abrupt ending of the story about the laughing man. Gwynn and Blotner are mistaken when they assert that this story marks "a complete change in theme and technique" from previous *New Yorker* contributions. Like both "Uncle Wiggily in Connecticut" and "Just Before the War with the Eskimos" (and also "Blue Melody"), "The Laughing Man" concerns the disillusioning effect upon a child of adult pettiness that the child cannot comprehend.

The precise motive for dramatizing these particular recollections, however, is obscure because Salinger does not make clear whether Gedsudski is aware of the effect that his abrupt ending of the fantastic tale has upon his young charges. If he is deliberately relieving his own frustrations through the process of displacement (by taking out upon the "Comanches" feelings that he cannot vent upon the girl who has caused them), Wiegand is correct in asserting that the tale-teller achieves a "sublimation in art." On the other hand, Hassan's explanation that art is powerless to heal is correct if Gedsudski's romantic frustration has caused him to eschew both romance and story-telling in the future. In either case, however, he is a man who will sacrifice children's feelings in order to salve his own wounds. We even wonder if Mary Hudson may not have broken with Gedsudski because she has detected beneath the mask of his superficial good-fellowship the inner ruthlessness that motivates the self-made man. If so, the story is actually a bitter fable of the disillusionment of misplaced hero-worship; and it is this interpretation that would make the story into the most effective account of youth's initiation into the disillusioning realities of life.

This interpretation is supported by an examination of the "epiphany" that occurs after the narrator leaves the bus and sees the piece of red tissue paper flapping against the lamppost. Since it is the sight of this discarded paper that recalls the laughing man's mask and not the abrupt ending of the story in the bus that sets the young narrator's teeth chattering, events in both Gedsudski's story and real life have combined to rip away a child's illusions about the world. The tone of the narration, however, contradicts the idea that the narrator has become disillusioned about Gedsudski, because even as a grown-up the narrator speaks so enthusiastically about Gedsudski that he seems as much a hero-worshipper when he tells the story as he was when he was nine. If the boy had been really disillusioned with Gedsudski, a more ironic tone should pervade his narration of the story. It is finally impossible to tell whether the intention is to exalt or expose Gedsudski. Possibly Salinger's feelings about his character are as ambivalent as Holden's about the movies; he may be fascinated by the very "phoniness" he wishes to detest.

IV *"Down at the Dinghy"*

No such ambiguity plagues Salinger's next published story, "Down at the Dinghy," which also describes the unpleasant impact of the adult world upon Lionel Tannenbaum, a boy who is even younger and less conscious of the source of his difficulties than the narrator of "The Laughing Man."

"Down at the Dinghy" is a brief and economically worded drama, played in two swift-moving scenes. The first provides the background for understanding the second. As the curtain rises—the dramatic metaphor is irresistible—we find a family maid discussing with a cleaning lady employed by the day the two sources of the maid's discomfort: her being held at the family's country home into October when she would prefer to be back in the city enjoying her social life, and her fear that the family's four-year-old son Lionel will tell something she has said. When the boy's twenty-five-year-old mother (who proves to be Seymour Glass's sister Boo Boo) enters, we learn that the boy has "run away" to a dinghy anchored in the lake at the edge of the property and also that he has run away in the city several times before when people have said things that have upset him.

In the second scene, Boo Boo, using an admirable form of non-directive counseling, finally induces Lionel to return home. After throwing his late Uncle Seymour's goggles into the lake and then punishing himself by also tossing in a coveted chain of keys, he breaks into tears and at last confesses that he has run away because he has heard the maid call his father "a big—sloppy—kike," which he supposes to mean "kite." After having been promised that he may go to the station to meet Daddy, he races his mother back to the house and wins.

The most comprehensive analysis of this delicately wrought vignette of the touchiness of upper-middle-class urban American society appears in a pamphlet of commentaries on modern American short stories prepared by John Edward Hardy to accompany a collection of stories in English for German students. Hardy begins his analysis by emphasizing—erroneously, I believe—its, concern with "the social problem of anti-Semitism in the United States." He finally admits, however, that it is not "*as* Jews that Boo Boo and her son are interesting and admirable, but merely as people." Thereafter he displays a sensitive perception of Salinger's expert portrayal of Boo Boo's expert handling of a hypersensitive child who cannot be "*forced into anything*." After showing how Boo Boo, while retaining control of the situation, allows Lionel "to assert his independence of her moral judgments" by punishing himself for spitefully throwing away his uncle's goggles, Hardy concludes that in the "symbolic race" at the end of the story, "*both* won," since, by letting Lionel win, Boo Boo "secured the victory, herself, with and for him."[3] Thus, as William Wiegand points out in a single-sentence criticism of the story, the point is that relief for the suffering of the hypersensitive individual may be provided by "the love and understanding of parents."

Little would need to be added to Hardy's analysis if he did not —like other critics—overstress the possible commentary on anti-Semitism. The story may not even deal with anti-Semitism in the conventional sense, since there is no reason to believe that the maid was not Jewish herself. Certainly there is no evidence that her only reported use of the word "kike" is not just an impulsive outburst rather than an expression of a long-standing prejudice. She has reasons to be in the kind of mood that would cause her to speak indiscreetly.

She is surely not well received by the working class in the region around the country house. She summarizes her situation when she says to the cleaning woman, "You got your social life here." The cleaning woman also nastily emphasizes that Sandra does not "belong" when she remarks that the maid can drink without difficulty tea hotter than the cleaning woman can drink at all. Sandra, herself the victim of provincial prejudice, could have said something that might injure others because she feels hurt herself.

The emphasis upon the story as a possible attack upon

prejudice would not matter—since the use of derogatory terms is surely one of the things that keeps the world from being "nice"—if it had not prevented commentators from seeing the significance that Lionel may be attaching to his own misconstruction of the overheard word. Since he does not as yet know what "kike" means, the term itself could not disturb him; but he might be quite upset if he supposed that his father were actually a "kite," which he defines as "one of those things that go up in the *air*" and is held with a string. Then Lionel might suppose that if the fragile string should slip from his hands or break—as kite strings often do—his father would "fly away."

Lionel is immensely *attached* to his father. One time when the boy intended to run away from the family's New York apartment, he got only to the front door of the building because he wanted to wait to say good-bye to his father. He covets the key chain because it is like his father's. He retreats to the dinghy because, as he emphasizes to his mother, it is his father's domain. The inaudibility of his voice when he names his father suggests that he is worried about him. If he is, the mother's promise at the end of the story that she will take Lionel to the station to meet Daddy and bring him home assumes a far greater significance than has usually been assigned to it. Like most boys who attempt to run away, the unusually sensitive Lionel probably suffers terrifying fears of being unwanted. To such a child the thought that his father was a "kite" would be as disturbing as would the term "kike" if he knew what it meant.

It is especially ironic that the situation with which the story deals has probably been brought about by the boy's penchant for running away. Although we do not know why the family has failed to move back to the city at the usual time, it could be to keep him from the great dangers to which he exposes himself when he runs away in Manhattan. His mother stresses that the park to which he fled one night was freezing cold and probably full of "roaming degenerates." The family's long stay in the country, however, both antagonizes the maid and keeps the commuting father from being home as much as usual during the hours that Lionel is awake, so that an ideal situation is provided for the making and misinterpreting of the maid's troublesome remark.

A remarkable quality of this short story is that almost nothing "happens" in it—the conflict is entirely verbal. Since Salinger has never mentioned James Joyce, it is not possible to tell what influence this important literary theorist may have had upon the younger writer; but "Uncle Wiggily in Connecticut," "Just Before the War with the Eskimos," and "The Laughing Man," although varying in quality, all serve to illustrate the Joycean concept, explained in *Stephen Hero,* of the "epiphany"—"a sudden spiritual manifestation, whether in the vulgarity of speech or of gesture or in a memorable phase of the mind itself."[4] We observe such manifestations in Eloise's impulsive caressing of Ramona's glasses, in Ginnie's renouncing her demands for the cab fare, and in the young narrator's reaction in "The Laughing Man" to the mask-like red paper around the lamppost.

"Down at the Dinghy" really marks the "change in technique" that Gwynn and Blotner perceived in "The Laughing Man," for it provides an example not of the story built around an "epiphany" but of the more complex theories of "tragic" or "dramatic" emotion that Stephen explains in Joyce's *A Portrait of the Artist as a Young Man.* Certainly "Down at the Dinghy" is a "static" story that inspires not the "desire and loathing" that Stephen associates with "improper arts," but instead the pity and terror which Stephen defines as follows:

—Pity is the feeling which arrests the mind in the presence of whatsoever is grave and constant in human suffering and unites it with the human sufferer. Terror is the feeling which arrests the mind in the presence of whatsoever is grave and constant in human suffering and unites it with the secret cause.[5]

Surely, as Salinger sees things, that which is grave and constant in human suffering is the fear of being misunderstood and unloved. In "Down at the Dinghy" pity is inspired by our union with a group of human sufferers—Sandra, cut off from her social life; Boo Boo, who finds her son's behavior "slightly over" her head; Lionel, the victim of an adult world whose language he does not understand. Terror is inspired by the reader's perception that the secret cause of this human suffering is what Gwynn and Blotner identify as a major aspect of the story, "the failure of communication."

V "For Esmé—with Love and Squalor"

"Down at the Dinghy" deals with a far more universal problem than the Jew's role in society; it is Salinger's presentation of the static essence of tragedy. His next story, "For Esmé—with Love and Squalor," which Gwynn and Blotner consider the "high point" of his art, is precisely the opposite: it is his dramatization of the dynamic essence of comedy, whose secret cause might be said to be the triumphant joy occasioned by a successful communication between human beings.

This story has been most accurately described by Ihab Hassan as a "modern epithalamium," written in honor of the wedding of an ideal woman and depicting the love that the narrator feels for her and the squalor that she has requested in the story he will write for her. Like "Down at the Dinghy," "For Esmé" unfolds—after a brief invocatory prologue that states, not entirely ironically, that the aim of the writer is not to please, but "to edify, to instruct"—in two brief scenes. The first provides the background for understanding the second. The technique of the story is awkward; at the beginning of the second part, Salinger—for reasons he is "not at liberty to disclose"—shifts the narration from first to third person. The reasons are not obvious, although they may only be that the American soldier who narrates the story would have been reluctant to discuss in the first person the squalid things that he discloses about himself and others in the second part of the story, in which he reappears as Sergeant X. The awkward juncture in the middle of the story, however, does not mar the overall effectiveness of the moving tale.

In the first scene, a titled British girl of about thirteen, whom the narrator has observed singing at a local choir rehearsal, sufficiently overcomes her aristocratic reserve to approach him and to talk to him in a tearoom. She displays a tremendous knack for "keeping count" of things, a desire to train herself to be more compassionate, and a contempt for Americans, since most she has met "act like animals." Among other things, she asks the American, when he tells her that he is a writer, to write a story just for her about "squalor," with which he ruefully acknowledges he is constantly becoming "better acquainted."

They are joined after a few minutes by Esmé's five-year-old brother, who laughs uproariously at his own riddles but who himself acts like an animal and stomps away infuriated when the narrator beats him to the punch line the second time the boy asks the same riddle. Esmé admits that her brother Charles has a violent temper; but at the end of the interview, she manages to drag the boy back to kiss the narrator good-bye (as decorum would not permit her to do herself). When the narrator asks the riddle and allows Charles to deliver the punch line, the boy rushes from the room, "possibly in hysterics." Esmé then takes a more formal and courteous departure, hoping that the narrator may return from the war with all his "faculties intact."

In the second scene, the narrator—now Sergeant X—has indeed become acquainted with squalor. Possibly to illustrate Esmé's statement that Americans "act like animals," which the narrator chided as snobbish, Salinger exhibits one of the most grotesque arrays of insensitive egotists ever assembled in such small compass. To set the tone, there is the lingering ghost of the vicious Nazi leader Joseph Goebbels, who, as Gwynn and Blotner point out in a long analysis, hated human beings. In *The Time Without Parallel,* a book by the monstrous Goebbels, the Nazi spinster whose former room Sergeant X occupies has scrawled, "Dear God, life is hell." The Sergeant glosses her statement by adding another from Dostoevski's *The Brothers Karamazov* about hell being "the suffering of being unable to love."

That the spirit of Goebbels has not been crushed in that the lovelessness of his "time" is regrettably paralleled by his conquerors is then demonstrated first by a sadistic letter from the Sergeant's older brother asking for "a couple of bayonets or swastikas" for his kids. Sergeant X tears up this letter and throws it into a wastebasket into which he later vomits, but he cannot easily escape the squalor personified by the "photogenic" Corporal Z, from whom we learn that the Sergeant has just been released from the hospital after a nervous breakdown.

The Corporal, whose first name is Clay (an inert, earthy name that could also echo one of James Joyce's most poignant tales of squalor), brings news of the officious Bulling, who forces underlings to travel at inconvenient hours in order to show his authority; of Clay's insensitive girl friend, Loretta, a psychology major, who blames Sergeant X's breakdown not on the war but on a lifelong instability and yet excuses Clay's sadistic killing of a cat as "temporary insanity" brought on by the war; and of his mother, who is glad that Clay has gone through the war with the Sergeant, because her son's letters have been "more intelligent" since the two men have been associated.

The most squalid of the lot, however, is Clay himself, a completely "hollow man," who will not even acknowledge that another is criticizing him. Sergeant X is finally exasperated beyond the bounds of his usual courtesy into a rare moment of truth by Clay's insistence upon dwelling on his sadistic act of killing the cat. The sergeant makes it clear that he thinks the Corporal has been "brutal," "cruel," and "dirty." Clay, however, who thinks Eisenhower jackets are good because they "look good," only asks why the Sergeant can't ever be "*sincere.*"

When Clay finally leaves, the Sergeant—who has thought better of apologizing to the callow young man—is too disturbed to type a letter that may have some slight therapeutic value. He closes his eyes, and upon reopening them finds a tiny package that has been following him for about a year. It is from Esmé, and it contains her father's watch, which she hopes the Sergeant will accept as "a lucky talisman." There is also a postscript of "hellos" from Charles, whom Esmé is "teaching to read and write and . . . finding an extremely intelligent novice." This unexpected act of unadulterated affection redeems the Sergeant from his private hell and enables him to go to sleep; he feels he may yet come through the war with his "faculties intact."

"For Esmé—with Love and Squalor" is thus a dramatic gloss on the Dostoevski quotation that the trembling Sergeant writes in Goebbels' book. Just before the appearance of his much acclaimed novel, *The Catcher in the Rye*, Salinger succeeded in creating in Esmé and in Corporal Clay perfect personifications of the "nice" and the "phony" worlds as he envisioned them; he also recorded one of the rare victories of the "nice" over the "phony."

Not even the most artfully contrived story, however, is immune from ingenious misreading. In "J. D. Salinger: Hello Hello Hello" (*College English*, January, 1961), John Hermann argues that Esmé herself is "the distillation of squalor" and that her brother Charles is "the key to the story." Fortunately Robert M. Browne rushed gallantly to Esmé's defense ("Rebuttal," *College English*, May, 1961); and, accurately charging Hermann with "the romantic preconception . . . that love of truth, including statistics, makes one unable to love people," refutes the earlier argument by pointing out, among other things, that Esmé clearly has to drag Charles back into the restaurant to kiss the narrator and that it is she who sends the Sergeant her dearest possession and writes the accompanying letter that carries Charles's cheery postscript. Browne could also have pointed out that she has even taught Charles to be able to write this postscript.

Even Browne fails, however, to recognize the importance of Charles in dramatizing the victory of the "nice" world in this story. As I have pointed out, Esmé acknowledges that Charles has a "furious temper" that makes him act like an animal—the way Americans act. Charles is a wild but inquisitive young animal who has lost—through the hell of the Nazi-inspired war—the kind of parental guidance which may redeem Lionel Tannenbaum, in "Down at the Dinghy," from his animalistic egotism. The story of Esmé thus records a double struggle—that not only for Sergeant X's soul, but also for Charles's. Can the boy be kept from becoming the kind of brutal and insensitive sadist that Corporal Z has become? Even though Esmé is still trying to teach herself compassion, she has assumed the burden of being her brother's keeper as well. She scores a small victory when she forces him to return to kiss the alien soldier whom he has fled in anger; she scores a greater victory when her "extremely intelligent novice" adds to her compassionate letter a string of "hello's" that marks the beginning of an ability to communicate successfully.

How conscious Salinger may have been that in this story he was actually paying tribute to the self-discipline that is in the best tradition of the British aristocracy cannot be gauged, but one point of the story is surely that one should not be put off by disciplined exteriors that conceal compassionate hearts, for they bring what love there is to a world made squalid by those, like Corporal Z, who conceal a spiritual void beneath a smiling, "photogenic" surface.

CHAPTER 8

The Artist as a Very
Nervous Young Man

I *A Gathering of Exegetes*

SO MUCH has already been written about *The Catcher in
the Rye* that it might appear unlikely that there is anything
left to say. Although the novel was not accorded as immediate
scholarly attention as James Gould Cozzens' *By Love Possessed*,
it has, since 1954, been the subject of probably more critical
pronouncements than any other postwar novel.

Despite readers' enthusiastic response to *Catcher*, the critical
chorus has generally been discordant. One thing, in fact, that
has tended to detract from Salinger's reputation is that only a
few of his ardent admirers have been heard from in print.
Henry Anatole Grunwald's *Salinger: A Critical and Personal
Portrait* (1962) anthologizes most of these comparatively few
"appreciations" in two sections entitled "Between Miracle and
Suicide" and "The Phoenix." Perhaps the most impressive is
Dan Wakefield's "Salinger and the Search for Love," originally
prepared for *New World Writing* (Number 14). Wakefield
speaks for most Salinger *aficionados* when he says that the
author "speaks for all who have not lost hope—or even if they
have lost hope, have not lost interest—in the search for love
and morality in the present-day world" and that Salinger is "the
only new writer to emerge in America since the second world
war who is writing on what has been the grandest theme of
literature: the relationship of man to God, or the lack of God"
(Grunwald, 178, 186).

Even more sweeping is Martin Green's claim, reproduced
from his book *A Mirror for Anglo-Saxons* (1960), that Salinger

is a cultural "image-maker," who provides in Holden Caulfield a kind of heroic figure to whom we all look up and in whom "Wellesley and Harvard undergraduates can recognize themselves transfigured, more intensely alive, more honest, more passionate, more courageous" (Grunwald, 253). Similar sentiments are expressed in an essay written by an undergraduate, Christopher Parker, for the anthology. Although Parker admits that most young men who read *Catcher*, "don't think about it enough—what's really behind it all," he says that we "can all identify ourselves" with Holden's plight (Grunwald, 258, 254).

A somewhat more sober approach is taken in the essay that signaled the beginning of academic attention to *Catcher*—Arthur Heiserman and James E. Miller, Jr.'s, "J. D. Salinger; Some Crazy Cliff," written as one of a series of "revaluations" for *Western Humanities Review* in 1956. The two authors attempt to place the novel in the mainstream of American and world fiction by showing its relationship to the "tradition of the quest," a preoccupation of the rising school of myth critics. The article especially endears itself to admirers of the book because of the authors' conclusion that "it is not Holden who should be examined for a sickness of the mind, but the world in which he sojourned and found himself an alien" (Grunwald, 205).

Most critics have not, however, been swayed by such passionate rhetoric. The first influential naysayer was Ernest Jones, Freud's student and biographer, who, in his review of the novel for the *Nation* (September 1, 1951, 176), provided an enduring catchphrase when he described *Catcher* as "a case history of all of us." The book, Jones says, is "not at all something rich and strange, but what every sensitive 16-year-old since Rousseau has felt, and of course what each of us is certain he has felt." The novel, as a result, although "lively in its parts," is "as a whole . . . predictable and boring." While Jones appears to be judging *Catcher* as a psychoanalytical document rather than as a work of art, his observation that Holden "mistakes whatever is spontaneous in his behavior for madness" is vital to an understanding that Holden is not a romantic rebel in the American transcendental tradition.

A far less justifiable conclusion is reached in the first discussion of *Catcher* in a book about contemporary American literature, John W. Aldridge's *In Search of Heresy* (1956). Seizing upon the comparison between Huck Finn and Holden, which has been carefully and thoughtfully explored by many writers (see essays by Charles Kaplan, Edgar Branch, and Alvin R. Wells listed in the bibliography), Aldridge argues that whereas Huck's innocence is "a compound of frontier ignorance, juvenile delinquency, and penny-dreadful heroism," Holden's is "a compound of urban intelligence, juvenile contempt, and *New Yorker* sentimentalism" (129-30). Arguing further that Holden never recognizes the phoniness that he objects to as "what one part of humanity *is*," Aldridge—who apparently has no concept of the moral complexity of urban life—reaches the conclusion to which many other critics have objected: that Holden "remains at the end what he was at the beginning—cynical, defiant, and blind" (131). Ihab Hassan dismisses these charges in *Radical Innocence* (1961), but he points out that among the novel's "real failings" are Holden's refusal "to draw any conclusions from his experience" and Salinger's failure to modify Holden's point of view by any other (275).

Maxwell Geismar in *American Moderns from Rebellion to Conformity* (1958) also takes Salinger to task for the lack of conclusions in the novel, which he describes as "the *New Yorker* school of ambiguous finality at its best" written by an "Exurbanite Radical Party of One." Acknowledging that *Catcher* protests "against both the academic and social conformity of its period," Geismar asks, "What does it argue *for* ?" Its real achievement, he thinks, "is that it manages so gracefully to evade just those central questions which it raises" (198). Still more disturbed about Salinger's lack of concern with "issues" is Barbara Giles, whose "The Lonely War of J. D. Salinger" (*Mainstream*, February, 1959) is the only discussion of Salinger's work I can locate in a journal of leftist opinion. She asks: "Is it a superior virtue to dream of rescuing imaginary children from a mythical danger instead of saving 'innocent guys'—real ones—from legalized death because the crusader can't be certain that his sword is untarnished by a fleck of exhibitionism?" (7).

Two other critics link Salinger with Jack Kerouac in expressing the suspicion that Holden's lack of meaningful rebellion is symptomatic of a decline in American frontier traditions. Leslie Fiedler in *Love and Death in the American Novel* (1960) comments that "whether on the upper-middle-brow level of Salinger or the Bohemian-*kitsch* level of Kerouac, such writers echo not the tragic *Huckleberry Finn*, but the sentimental book with which it is interwined" (271). More barbed than Fiedler's truncheons are the words wielded to like effect by Kingsley Widmer, who, in "The American Road" (*University of Kansas City Review,* June, 1960) points out that in both *Catcher* and *On the Road,* "we find much the same messianic yearnings" of heroes "who repeatedly get bailed out before fully engaging their own experience and the consequences." Although earlier the "road" had been "the way of honor . . . and initiation . . . of the archetypal American hero," Holden does not really "break into freedom," but only "ritualistically *plays* at the big-boy's kind of freedom just to neutralize and dispel it for easier adjustment" (307, 313-14).

Another group of ill-disposed critics has sought to account for the popularity of *Catcher.* Frank Kermode, in "Fit Audience" (*Spectator,* May 30, 1958), argues that Holden's "attitudes to religion, authority, art, sex, and so on are what smart people would like other people to have, but cannot have themselves because of superior understanding." Thus he believes that Salinger's success "springs from his having, with perfect understanding supplied their demand for this kind of satisfaction" (705). His charges are augmented by Alfred Kazin's observation in a *Harper's* special supplement on "Writing in America" (October, 1959, p. 130) that Salinger lacks strength because "he identifies himself too fussily with the spiritual aches and pains of his characters" and exemplifies the writer who is "reduced to . . . the 'mystery of personality' instead of the drama of our social existence." Writing the next month about "The Salinger Industry" in the *Nation* (November 14, 1959, pp. 360-63), George Steiner (author of the widely acclaimed *Tolstoy or Dostoevsky?* and *The Death of Tragedy*) stridently appointed himself to command of the anti-Salinger forces by charging that the novelist's "semi-literate maunderings of the adolescent mind" flattered "the very ignorance and shallowness of his young readers." Salinger, Steiner continued, depicted as "positive virtues": "formal ignorance, political apathy, and a vague *tristesse.*" The "industry" that had promoted Salinger to the ranks of the great writers, Steiner attributed to American academic critics who cannot write "with plainness or understatement," who are under "undue pressure to publish," and who, therefore, do not carry out the critic's proper task of distinguishing "what is great from what is competent."

Part of Steiner's essay and other examples of recent sniping at Salinger may be found in that section of Grunwald's *Salinger* titled "Magician, Clubman, or Guru." It contains, for example, David Leitch's attribution in "The Salinger Myth" of the novelist's influence to the prevalence of the type of person "young, or obsessed with youth" and "profoundly conscious of being set apart from the run-of-the-mill human beings he sees around him," who considers "communication with outsiders . . . not only useless but impossible," and "apt, if attempted, to cause unpleasant situations" (Grunwald, 70-71).

Despite the vast amount of writing about *The Catcher in the Rye*, there have been remarkably few articles that have attempted simply to analyze the novel without excessively praising the author or picking a quarrel with him. Frederick Gwynn and Joseph Blotner in *The Fiction of J. D. Salinger* (1958; largely reprinted in Grunwald, *Salinger*), the first monograph about the novelist, analyze many short stories in detail, but spend little time on the novel. They do draw a forced comparison between Holden and Jesus; but this attempt to climb on the critically fashionable bandwagon with those who find a passion legend in every tale of individual tribulation obliges the collaborators to confuse compassionate forgiveness with adolescent nostalgia. The discussion closes with the unwarranted statement that the novel's conclusion is "just as artistically weak— and as humanly satisfying—as that of *Huckleberry Finn*," probably because to round off their parallel Holden would have to be "crucified," as Jim Casy is in *The Grapes of Wrath*.

The most useful article written about *Catcher* is Donald Costello's "The Language of *The Catcher in the Rye*," which Grunwald naïvely treats as an example of the lengths to which "earnest scholarship can go." Costello identifies the specific ingredients of the "type of informal, colloquial teenage American speech" used in the novel, to which many critics had paid vague tributes. He also catalogues and provides specific examples of the devices Salinger uses to characterize Holden individually (ending sentences with "and all," "I really did," "if you want to know the truth"), and also as a typical teen-ager of his time (crude language, slang, trite figures of speech, use of nouns as adjectives, adverbs) (Grunwald, *Salinger*, pp. 266-76).

The only really objective analysis of *Catcher* and the most ambitious discussion of the novel written thus far is Carl F.

Strauch's "Kings in the Back Row: Meaning through Structure" (*Wisconsin Studies in Contemporary Literature,* Winter, 1961). Arguing from the premise that "structure *is* meaning," Strauch points out that "except in scattered and fragmentary flashes, it has thus far escaped attention that Salinger sharply accentuates the portrayal of Holden with a symbolic structure of language, motif, episode, and character" (6). He attempts to rectify this situation by an explanation of "the interlocking metaphorical structure" of the novel, which allows us to perceive that "Salinger has employed neurotic deterioration, symbolic death, spiritual awakening, and psychological self-cure as the inspiration and burden of an elaborate pattern" (7).

Although Strauch's theory that "Holden psychologically dies only to be reborn into the world of Phoebe's innocence and love" and then effects "his own psychological regeneration" leads to subtle insights into Holden's language ("slob" for the public world, "literate" for his private world) and into the imagery of the novel, it leads also to the untenable conclusion that the end of the novel is "blunted . . . because we cannot say what society will do to impose adjustment upon a body who has effected his own secret cure" (27). The trouble with this conclusion is that, if Holden has really effected his own cure, society will not be able to "impose" anything upon him; for he will have prepared himself to meet its demands. The end of the novel could not then be "blunted," for Holden's subsequent career would be too obvious to be depicted. Strauch strains too hard to make the novel conform to a single narrative pattern. He does not, therefore, either elucidate the complex interweaving of several narrative strands in the novel or discern how the conclusion provides a complete and satisfactory resolution of these strands.

II *The Catcher in the Rye—Search for Tranquillity*

To determine the exact relationship to an overall pattern of each detail in the novel would require a book as long as the novel itself. It is possible, however, to provide a more complete structural analysis of *The Catcher in the Rye* than has previously appeared by outlining the three main patterns that must be considered in interpreting the work.

Although *Catcher* is richly and elaborately embellished, it is basically the account of the breakdown of a sixteen-year-old boy. The novel does not attempt to trace the whole history of this catastrophe from its origins, but concentrates on the events of its critical stage. Salinger tries hard to make clear just what he is doing when he has Holden comment that "all that David Copperfield kind of crap" bores him and that he is going to tell only "about this madman stuff" that happened just before he got "pretty run-down" (3).*

Even though Holden acknowledges being attended by a psychoanalyst at the end of the book, his breakdown is clearly not just—or even principally—mental. He is physically ill. He has grown six and a half inches in a year and "practically got T. B." (8). He also admits that he is "skinny" and has not kept to the diet that he should to gain weight (140). He is passing through the most physically difficult period of adolescence when only the most sympathetic care can enable the body to cope with the changes it is undergoing.

Holden's condition is complicated, however, by emotional problems. His mother is ill and nervous, and his father is so busy being successful that he never discusses things with his son (140). Holden is thus without the kind of parental guidance an adolescent urgently needs during this crucial period. The school to which he has been packed off fails to take the place of his parents. Holden's complaint is not that Pencey Prep—like schools in European novels such as Sybille Bedford's *A Legacy* or even the monstrous American military academy in Calder Willingham's *End As a Man*—is overbearing or destructive of individuality, but rather that "they don't do any damn more molding at Pencey than they do at any other school" (4). While the administrators entertain prospective donors, the kind of cliques of hoodlums that drive James Castle to suicide operate unchecked. Although Holden is trying to cling to an unrealistically rigid Victorian moral code, he also lacks what David Riesman calls the "psychological gyroscope" that keeps the "inner-directed" personality on course. (To classify Holden in the terms provided by *The Lonely Crowd*, he is an "inner-directed" personality in an "other-directed" society—an unhappy

---

* Figures in parentheses throughout this chapter refer to page numbers in the original edition of *The Catcher in the Rye* (Boston: Little, Brown, 1951). This same pagination is preserved in the undated Modern Library edition and also in the Grosset and Dunlap reprint.

phenomenon so common today that it alone could account for many persons' identification with Holden.)

Holden also has the intellectual problem of preparing himself for a vocation, because he rejects the kind of career for which his schooling is preparing him and as yet he can conceive of no realistic substitute for it. His emotional and intellectual problems do not, however, cause his breakdown; rather his rundown physical condition magnifies the pain these problems cause him. The boy is struggling, without enlightened assistance, against greater odds than he can fight for himself; and his "quest" during the critical period described in the book is not really for some metaphysical "grail" but simply for a "nice" (he uses the word himself at the end of his adventures, p. 275) refuge from the "phony" world that threatens to engulf him.

Those who find the book nothing more than a satirical attack upon the "phoniness" that irritates Holden's condition are probably as disturbed as the boy himself; for—as Marc Rosenberg points out—Holden suffers because of an undisciplined hypersensitivity.[1] The most common complaint that cooler and supposedly wiser heads like Ernest Havemann[2] level at the novel is that Holden is himself guilty of all the things that make him call others "phony." As Christopher Parker admits, the charge is absolutely true.[3] In the opening chapters of the novel, Salinger strains to make it clear that Holden does precisely what he objects to other people's doing. He displays the vain irresponsibility that he criticizes in "secret slob" Stradlater (35) when he loses the fencing team's equipment (6). He stands in another's light just as he complains Ackley does (40, 28). He lectures Ackley in the same way that he objects to the history teacher's lecturing him (32, 16-17). Like Ackley, he will do what others want only when he is shouted at (32, 63). Like Luce, he will discuss only what he feels like talking about (188, 71). He is especially guilty of overgeneralizing. Although he complains that everybody—especially his father—"think something's all true" when it's only partly true, he ends the very paragraph in which he makes this charge with his own generalization that "people never notice anything" (13). Elsewhere he comments—to cite only a few examples—"people never believe you" (48), women always leave bags in the aisle (70), "all those Ivy League bastards look alike" (112).

There is no point in multiplying examples; Holden obviously

fails to see that his criticisms apply to himself. If, however, we think that his failure to practice what he preaches invalidates his criticisms, we fall into an *argumentum ad hominem*—we cannot justify our shortcomings by pointing the finger of scorn at our critics, especially if we do not wish to admit that we are as sick as they are. Like many sensitive but immature people, Holden is not yet well enough in control of his faculties to see the application of his strictures to himself. As Ihab Hassan warns, there is as great a danger "in taking Holden at his word as in totally discounting his claim."[4] Despite Martin Green's claims, Salinger is not offering Holden to the world as an example of what it should be.[5] If those who think that Holden could pull himself together if he would just "try" are as insensitive as the people who fail Holden in the novel, those who make a martyr of Holden are victims of the same immature hypersensitivity that he is. Both make the mistake of supposing that the novel is what Ernest Jones calls "a case history of all of us." It is not; there are adolescents like those Holden says are "as sensitive as a goddam toilet seat" (72); there are those who are driven to suicide by their real or imagined tormentors (like James Castle or Seymour Glass); and there are sensitive ones who are saved by a stronger sense of "inner direction" than Holden possesses. The popularity of the novel suggests, however, that fully literate youth in our society finds it especially easy to identify with Holden.

Many people who read too much of themselves into the novel do not seem to realize that Holden is not seeking admiration, but the understanding that will help him through a difficult period. (When Phoebe does dramatically show admiration for him by insisting upon running away with him, he realizes that he cannot accept the responsibility of hero-worship.) He is not—like most restless rebels in American literature (Leatherstocking, Ahab, Carol Kennicott, Arrowsmith, Clyde Griffiths, Danny in *Tortilla Flat*, Dean Moriarity, Henry Miller in *Tropic of Cancer*, even Nick Carraway, until he is disillusioned)—seeking to run away from a monotonous, humdrum life, but to run toward some kind of tranquil sanctuary. It has not even been generally observed that Holden does not even consider "running away" from urban society until very near the end of the book, and that he leaves school early and goes to New York City so that he can hibernate in a cheap hotel room and "go home all rested up and feeling swell" (66). He cannot carry out this plan, however, because he cannot stand being alone; he feels like "giving somebody a buzz" as soon as he hits town. If he were not constantly seeking company, he might have to think about his situation and his experiences, but he is not yet ready to accept this demanding intellectual responsibility.

He needs sympathy, and he has not been able to find it at school. His history instructor lectures him about things he already knows, but he cannot answer the one question that Holden plaintively asks—"Everybody goes through phases and all, don't they?" (21). His schoolmates aggravate his condition: Ackley will move only if yelled at; Stradlater is not interested in a person's "lousy childhood," but only "very sexy stuff" (42). Both give Holden "a royal pain" by running down the few accomplishments that may give other people some vitally needed self-confidence (37). When Holden yells, *"Sleep tight, ya morons!"* as he leaves Pencey (68), he probably does not fully understand his own motives, but he senses that those he leaves behind are sleeping morons because they are too obsessed with their own nose drops, pimples, and good looks even to be interested in trying to figure out what may really be troubling a boy who they know is flunking out. (Holden, of course, does not try to figure out what their problems are, but he is at least sometimes aware that he does not know all about people. His immediate problem, furthermore, is more urgent than theirs.)

Holden fares no better in New York City. Readers who tend to idealize him should notice that his failures generally result from his own desperate impetuousness. When he first fails to arrange a rendezvous with the "available" Faith Cavendish, he acknowledges that he "fouled that up" (86). Although he finds one of the girls from Seattle whom he meets in the Lavender Room of his hotel to be a marvelous dancer, he snobbishly rejects all of them because "they don't know any better" than to drink Tom Collinses in the middle of December (97) or to go to Radio City Music Hall (98), where he subsequently goes himself. He irritates a touchy taxi driver with questions about the ducks in Central Park (107-8), and he leaves a night club because he doesn't want to be "bored to death" by an old flame of his brother's and her naval officer escort (114).

Although it is "against his principles," he allows Maurice, an elevator operator, to send a prostitute to his room (119). Feeling "much more depressed than sexy," he attempts to engage the unwilling girl in conversation (123). When he refuses to pay an extra five dollars that she and the pimp try to bilk him of, he is beaten up, although his plaint is only that "it'd be different" if they had asked for ten dollars to begin with (134). His old girl friend, Sally Hayes, actually proves no more understanding than the prostitute. Sally has evidently made her adjustment to the sophisticated life Holden hates. When he asks her if she hates school, she replies that "it's a terrific *bore*," but she doesn't "exactly *hate* it" (169). When he pleads with her to run away to the woods with him, she tries to "reason" with him by pointing out that his idea is "fantastic" and that there will be "oodles of marvelous places to go" if they get married after he finishes college (172). When he tells her that she gives him "a royal pain," she leaves in tears, and Holden rationalizes that he probably would not have taken her with him anyway (173-74). Obviously, from the way Sally attempts to change the subject from hating school and phonies, she cannot possibly help Holden because her own adjustment is still too precarious. Although she agrees that Holden is in "*lousy* shape," she cannot provide the understanding he needs.

Turning to a more mature ex-schoolmate, now a student at Columbia, Holden draws another blank. Carl Luce avoids discussion of the questions that most disturb Holden and finally coldly advises that the boy see a psychiatrist. A prototype of Lane Coutell in "Franny," Luce is described by Holden as one of those intellectuals who "don't like to have an intellectual conversation with you unless they're running the whole thing" (191). There is no aid for the bewildered in such monomaniacal monologues.

Finally, in the often-discussed scene in the Antolini apartment, Holden turns to a still older person, a respected teacher. Although Antolini does not mind being disturbed late at night and offers Holden a refuge, even this well-intentioned man fails as abysmally as the others to provide what the boy needs. After lecturing Holden at great length about not dying nobly for a cause, but living humbly for it—especially by applying one's self in school—Antolini wakes the boy who has at last gone to sleep by stroking him on the head. Much comment has been made about the soundness of Antolini's advice, which some critics think would have saved Holden, and also about Antolini's real intentions toward the boy, who jumps to the conclusion that the man who has appeared to be his last refuge from a "phony" world is making a homosexual advance toward him.

As far as the second matter goes, Salinger does not provide enough evidence to confirm or deny Holden's assumption. Although the teacher's calling Holden "handsome" and saying that he has been sitting "admiring" him arouse suspicion, his specific intentions are really beside the point. What matters is that he is guilty of a seriously faulty judgment; for, if he had perceived the depth of the boy's disturbance, he would have done nothing that might puzzle or upset him. By the time Holden reaches Antolini's, he is nearly at the breaking point. He not only yawns rudely in the man's face, but he contradicts himself several times. He says, for example, that an instructor at Pencey Prep "was intelligent and all, but you could tell he didn't have too much brains" (240). He also insists that "there were a couple of [classes] I didn't attend once in a while . . . but I didn't cut any" (242). If Antolini were really sensitive to another's condition, he would have noted these danger signals and left the boy strictly alone until the crisis had past; but, boozed up and enraptured by the sound of his own rhetoric, the "instructor" rattles on. Whatever his sexual propensities, his insensitivity drives the boy from his last refuge.

Antolini's behavior also casts doubt on the wisdom of his advice. Many writers have praised what he tells Holden because they agree with it; but this doesn't mean that Salinger does. Holden keeps the card upon which Antolini writes Stekel's advice about living humbly for a cause, but he may do this simply out of politeness or sentiment. Certainly when, a little later, he passes through his crisis, he does not recall the advice. What he wants from Antolini at the time he visits him is not more advice, but some kind of a gesture. Antolini makes a gesture all right, but an unfortunate one. Holden has come for understanding and receives instead the kind of lecture that Polonius delivers to Laertes in *Hamlet* before the son leaves home. And we know exactly what Holden thinks about this advice, for earlier in the book he has referred to the speech specifically as "the bull his father was shooting" (153). While it is dangerous to interpret an earlier work in the light of a later, we should at least recall, in considering Salinger's concept of Antolini, that many of the

novelist's later works have been devoted to the celebration of
Seymour Glass, who does not live humbly, but dies conspicuously, "dazzled to death by his own scruples."⁶

Certainly, whatever the value of Antolini's advice, Holden's
last hope in the world of his peers and elders has failed him;
he can turn only—as he has in moments of reverie throughout
the book—to the unchanging dead, to the memory of his brother
Allie, and it is Allie whom he addresses as his physical breakdown approaches its crisis. Walking along the street alone,
Holden pleads with Allie not to let him "disappear." Holden
survives, and only after this crisis has passed—as he is sitting
on a bench somewhere in the Sixties, breathless and sweating
(257)—does he decide that he will run away, pretend to be a
deaf mute, and hide his children. Society has failed him.

This decision climaxes the story of the disturbed boy's search
for understanding. All of his requests for assistance have failed;
he can now be redeemed only by an unsolicited gesture. This is
made by his little sister Phoebe, who—when she learns that
he plans to run away—insists on accompanying him. In the
meantime, Holden has discovered obscene words scribbled not
only in Phoebe's school, but in the almost sacred halls of the
Museum of Natural History, and he has realized that "you
can't ever find a place that's nice and peaceful, because there
isn't any" (264). He has resigned himself to the phoniness of the
world; and as far as he himself is concerned, he can simply
renounce it. When Phoebe insists on running away with
him, however, he realizes that he cannot take the responsibility
for her, because he will be depriving her of too many of the
opportunities open to her. He is most angry because if she runs
away with him, she won't be in the school play (274).

He decides that he must go home, not for his own sake, but
for Phoebe's; and lest the skeptical reader misinterpret his
intention, he emphasizes, "I really did go home afterwards"
(274). He manages, too, to reconcile Phoebe to accepting his
decision, not by pounding her ear, but by leaving her alone
until she is willing to respond to him. Having made and also
elicited a gesture of submission, Holden is rewarded at last
with the peace that he has sought, in the sight of Phoebe going
around and around on the carousel. He does not understand
why the sight makes him so happy; "it was just that she looked
so damn *nice*" (275). Eventually, of course, the carousel will

stop and Holden and Phoebe will have to return to the world that is "going somewhere"; but since there is no place that is permanently "nice and peaceful" in this world, these few minutes of aimless joy are the best that life affords.

This resolution of Holden's quest for physical tranquillity does not bring us to the end of the book, however, but only to the end of the penultimate chapter in which the climax of this strand of the narrative occurs and Phoebe's spontaneous gesture of affection produces a happier ending than might have been anticipated. Is the last brief chapter that closes the "frame" around Holden's account of his experience simply a tacked-on recital of "what came afterwards" in the tradition of the nine-teenth-century novel? If the novel were only the story of the overstrained Holden's search for something "nice" in a phony world, it would end with his admiring Phoebe riding the carousel.

III *The Catcher in the Rye—*
The Growth of Compassion

Another story, however, is intertwined with that of Holden's physical breakdown—the story of the breaking down of Holden's self-centeredness and his gradual acceptance of the world that has rejected him. Actually there is less development in this subplot than the other, because as the book opens Holden is already well on the road to countering his own phoniness with a kind of undiscriminating, universal love. As much as he detests some things about Ackley, he admits that he has to feel sorry for him (51). He also admits that whenever he is given a present, he ends up feeling sad (67). On the train to New York, instead of brooding over his own injuries, he concocts a tale that will make the mother of one of the "ratty" boys at Pencey Prep think well of her son (74): Unlike Ackley and Stradlater, he is not eager to minimize other youths' accomplishments.

In New York, the more he is hurt, the sorrier he feels for others. Even though he does not like the girl whose presence makes him leave the night club, he feels "sort of sorry for her, in a way" (113). He is still a virgin, because whenever he has tried to "make out" with girls and has been told to stop, he has stopped because he gets to "feeling sorry for them" (121). He even feels sorry for Jesus because the disciples let him down. Significantly, Holden supposes that the disciples proved

a disappointment because Jesus had to pick them *"at random"*
and "didn't have time to go around analyzing everybody" (130-
31). While waiting for Sally Hayes, Holden supposes that most
girls will get married to "dopey," "boring" men, but he admits
that he has to be careful about "calling certain guys bores,"
because he doesn't understand them (that is, he doesn't have
time to go around analyzing them.) He recalls one boring
roommate who was a terrific whistler and wonders if "maybe
they're secretly all terrific whistlers or something" (160-61).
During his interview with Antolini, Holden also admits that he
doesn't "hate too many guys" and that, when he does hate
people, "it doesn't last too long." If he doesn't see people for a
while, he "sort of" misses them (243). Antolini—like the history
teacher at Pencey Prep—is not ready, however, to follow up this
line of discussion which particularly concerns Holden. Antolini
sits silent for a while and then—although Holden wishes he
would postpone the discussion until morning—plunges again
into what he has on *his* mind.

The climax of the story of the internal development that
accompanies Holden's external breakdown occurs only a few
minutes before his climactic decision to run away. Awakening
from a nap on a bench in Grand Central Station, he thinks
over what happened in Antolini's apartment and wonders if
"just maybe" he was wrong in thinking that Antolini "was making
a flitty pass." Maybe Antolini "just liked to pat guys on the
head when they're asleep." Asking himself, "how can you tell
about that stuff for sure?," he replies, "You can't" (253). This
answer leads directly to the conclusion of the book, in which
Holden reports that he has begun to "miss" everybody he has
written about, even those that he has "hated" most—Stradlater,
Ackley, and worst of all, Maurice, the dishonest and brutal
elevator operator. In the light of what Holden told Antolini,
his "missing" them indicates that he no longer "hates" them,
because they, too, need understanding. Even Maurice, who has
hurt him most seriously, is a pathetic figure, who—if Holden's
prediction is true—will in a few years be "one of those scraggy
guys that come up to you on the street and ask for a dime for
coffee" (135). Recalling his own sufferings, Holden develops a
profound sense of the human condition lying behind the injunction that we must all love each other.

The brief concluding chapter in which this point is made

does not seem too well integrated into the novel because the idea of universal compassion—as Salinger handles it—is not too convincingly presented. Having recognized that the "nice" world of his dreams does not really exist, Holden seems unwilling to make any distinctions within the "phony" world. The implication of Holden's last statement grouping Ackley and Maurice with the less offensive people that Holden has met is that one is either phony or not; and since all are phony, all must be accepted equally. When one asks why comparative judgments may not be made, one finds—in the passage about Jesus and the disciples—only the somewhat lazy-minded explanation that one doesn't have time "to go around analyzing everybody." Holden's curious notion that Jesus picked the disciples at random can only reflect his own thinking about the way he would undertake such a task. Holden's impatience with taking the necessary time to make proper judgments also explains his advice at the end of the book, "don't ever tell anybody anything," for then one begins missing people (277). Since value judgments are complex and difficult to make, the best thing to do is to avoid them altogether. Holden's brand of "universal sympathy" seems less attractive when seen as the kind of two-valued "either . . . or" thinking which is the refuge of lazy minds. It is to this flabby aspect of Holden's thought that R. G. G. Price objects in *Punch* when he implies that Americans have a hard surface and a soft core.[7] With his swearing and swaggering, Holden exhibits a hard surface; but his refusal to make judgments—to speculate about motives—is indicative of a soft, sentimental core—and soft cores rot easily.

The trouble with this kind of sentimentality has been pointed out by William Wiegand in "J. D. Salinger: Seventy-Eight Bananas," and it is evident that Holden is an even more perfect exemplar than Seymour Glass of banana-fish fever. People must learn to make distinctions not because they should consistently follow some set of ethical principles, but simply because they are incapable of absorbing and retaining every experience. As Wiegand points out, Holden's trouble is that "he has no capacity to purge his sensations. He is blown up like a balloon, or like a bananafish, with his memories. Thus with the good things he remembers . . . he retains the bad things as well—until nothing is either good or bad after a point, but simply retained and cherished as a part of himself, submerging him with the sheer weight of accumulated burden."8

If the individual is submerged in this flux of undifferentiated experience, he can never hope to make his way toward any goal. The purpose of education should not be—as Antolini suggests in the novel—to give the individual an idea "what kind of thoughts [his] particular size mind should be wearing" (247), but to provide the individual with the tools for discriminating between experiences. As long as Holden has no wish to discriminate, he cannot possibly derive anything from attending classes. The reason he cannot tell the psychiatrist whether or not he is going to "apply" himself when he returns to school is that he still does not know *why* he is going to school or *why* he might wish to apply himself. He will continue to excel only in classes—like English composition—that may offer him a chance to express himself uncritically. The trouble with compassion is that, although without it one cannot be a decent human being, it cannot by itself provide a person with the means of making himself useful—as Holden learns when one of his most beautiful illusions is blasted. Being simply a saint requires no education.

IV *The Catcher in the Rye—Artist in Embryo*

Mention of Holden's lack of occupation brings us at last to the question of his "growing up" not physically (which is causing him pain) or emotionally (as he is doing when he rails against the kind of preconceived biases that make Catholics, intellectuals, bridge-players, and Book-of-the-Month Club members league snobbishly together [p.170]), but intellectually. A principal reason why Holden is having special difficulty while he is undergoing the physical changes leading to maturity and why he inclines towards a flabby sentimentality is that he does not wish to grow up because he sees no role for himself in the adult world.

What he considers especially "phony" is revealed in his conversation with Sally Hayes after he tells her, "I hate living in New York and all" (169). The "all" turns out to include such accouterments of urban life as "taxicabs, and Madison Avenue buses . . . and being introduced to phony guys that call the Lunts angels, and going up and down in elevators when you just want to go outside, and guys fitting your pants all the time at Brooks. . . ." He associates this life with his successful lawyer-father, who flies to California instead of attending Phoebe's play (210). Part of Holden's hatred of school stems from his unarticulated feeling that, if he ever finishes prep school, he may have to enter a hated Ivy League college and then take his place in the "ratrace." That in time he will is evident from the fact that he is no rebel. Whatever Holden wants, he does not wish to overthrow society. His question about everybody "going through phases" and even his undiscriminating love are evidences that he does not wish to be different from other people. As Hugh MacLean points out in "Conservatism in Modern American Fiction," Holden is a conservative[9]—partly because he accepts uncritically certain prejudices of his class and partly because he does not have the nerve to be anything else.

Examples of his unconscious acceptance of the prejudices of the urban upper-middle class are found in his criticism of the girls from Seattle who "didn't know any better" than to drink Tom Collinses in December (97), in his refusal to wear his beloved red hunting cap into the hotel because he doesn't want "to look like a screwball or something" (79), in his acknowledgment that he rooms with Stradlater because they both have good luggage (142), in his statement that he never says "crude things" to girls (178), and, most important of all, in his constantly displaying the trait of describing whatever is spontaneous in his behavior as "mad," because "everybody"—by which Holden means his father—has told him that he acts as if he were "only about twelve" (13).

His fear of asserting himself is much more strongly emphasized in the book than are his middle-class prejudices. He admits to Phoebe, for example, that "he was too yellow not to join" a secret fraternity at school (217). He also didn't have "the guts" to exact justice from the boy who stole his gloves (116). "If you want to stay alive," he observes on another occasion, you've got to say "stuff" like "glad to've met you" to people you aren't glad to have met (114). He is afraid that Sally Hayes will tell her father what Holden has called her (173). Also in the famous statement, which some people have tried to fling back into Salinger's face, about calling up the author of a book that "knocks you out," Holden says, "you wish that the author *was a terrific friend of yours* and you could call him up on the phone whenever you felt like it" (25, italics mine). Holden does not even think about calling up authors he does not know; he is not pushy.

Holden rejects not only rebellion, but also suicide. He is too "yellow" even to follow Seymour Glass and Teddy into the oblivion that will end his troubles. The one time he contemplates suicide, he fears that he might not be covered up right away and he doesn't want "a bunch of stupid rubbernecks" looking at him when he is "all gory" (136).

If one neither wishes to change and grow up, to run away, or to end it all, there remains only the conservative alternative of wishing that things would remain static and trying to keep them that way. This Holden adopts. "Certain things they should stay the way they are," he says in one of the few positive statements of belief he makes (158). Immediately before making this statement he has expressed his tremendous admiration for the lifelike exhibits in the New York Museum of Natural History, because "the best thing . . . in that museum was that everything always stayed right where it was." He observes sadly that on successive visits to the museum, "the only thing that would be different would be *you*" (157-58).

This desire to keep things exactly as they are inspires what is probably the most often quoted passage in the novel—the one which provides its title—in which Holden confesses to Phoebe his desire to be a "catcher in the rye" who would stand on the edge of "some crazy cliff" and catch the little kids "if they start to go over" (224). Although this "crazy cliff" may be identified in many ways, it is most obviously the border between the carefree innocence of childhood and the phony adult world that Holden himself does not wish to enter. His only ambition is the completely unrealistic one of keeping children from growing up.

Some readers—like John Aldridge—think that the book ends with Holden clinging to this forlorn hope. The climax of this strand of the narrative occurs, however, a little after those of the other two, in the same twenty-fifth chapter in which all of the intertwined histories are resolved. Many have objected to the vulgar language of *Catcher,* especially to the use of the word that Holden finds scrawled on the schoolroom and museum walls. The word is not employed, however—as stupid people suppose artists use words—so that the writer can see how much he can get away with, but because it is demanded by the structure of the story. Salinger's very point is that we cannot pretend that the word is not there by refusing to look at .it, for it is written even on the walls of the buildings where small children go to be educated.

The word is there, so that Holden—in an attempt to play the role that he has envisioned for himself as a "catcher in the rye"— may attempt to erase it. Its use is essential to Salinger's point. We must know what the word is to understand why Holden, in addition to erasing it the first time he sees it, has a fantasy of catching the person who wrote it on the wall and smashing "his head on the stone steps till he was good and goddam dead and bloody." Holden's dream of playing protector of the innocent leads to his climactic recognition of his own incapacity. Abandoning his fantasy, he says sadly, "I knew, too, I wouldn't have the guts to do it . . . I hardly even had the guts to rub it off the wall with my *hand*, if you want to know the truth. I was afraid some teacher would catch me rubbing it off and would think I'd written it" (261).

Yet he does erase the words; he finds them again, however, scratched into the wall. Then he recognizes sadly that "if you had a million years to do it in, you couldn't rub out even half" of the dirty symbols of the phony adult world that lead little children to the edge of "some crazy cliff" (262). After seeing the third of these signs Holden has a bowel movement (a rather literal symbol of catharsis) and then faints (265). Although he thinks that he could have killed himself, he hasn't. Rather he feels "better" after passing out. We need not look far for the symbolism of this passage. Holden himself has fallen over the "crazy cliff," but he is not destroyed—rather he feels better for being purged of the fantasies that tortured him.

That he has been changed is obvious from a passage near the end of the twenty-fifth chapter. After Holden puts Phoebe on the carousel, all the kids—including her—keep "trying to grab for the gold ring." Holden worries that Phoebe will "fall off," but he says nothing. "The thing with kids is," he observes, "if they want to grab for the gold ring, you have to let them do it, and not say anything. If they fall off, they fall off, but it's bad if you say anything to them" (273-74). This statement has a double significance. First, it shows that Holden no longer sees himself as a catcher in the rye. People will imitate others and grab for the gold ring, and "if they fall off, they fall off." He has resigned himself to the realities of human behavior. Second, the statement answers Antolini, who spoke of "a special kind of fall, a horrible kind" (243). He tries to talk Holden out of suffering this fall; but Holden finally finds the words with which he should have answered Antolini when he says that if kids "want to grab for the gold ring, you have to let them do it. . . . It's bad if you say anything to them." One must learn about life for himself. While academicians who are sympathetic with Antolini's viewpoint may think that his advice could have saved Holden, Holden could have taken the advice only if he had been a different person, heading for a different goal, in a differently structured book. *The Catcher in the Rye* is the story of a man who is not going to be saved by lectures.

His dreams of being a catcher shattered, is Holden left totally at loose ends? I think not. There are clues throughout the book that there is something he could be if he wished. In the description of his train trip to New York, Holden says that he had the woman to whom he was speaking "in a trance" and that he could "go on lying for hours" (73, 76). His "lies," of course, are pleasant fictions that he is inventing to delight his audience. In another place, Holden says self-mockingly, "All I need's an audience. I'm an exhibitionist" (38). He is closer to the truth than he realizes. He also unemphatically discloses that he is a good dancer (93) and a good golfer (100), and he insists on Phoebe's participating in the school play.

His attitude toward the movies is especially ambivalent. His judgment that his brother D. B. is "prostituting" himself in Hollywood (4), for example, shows Holden does "hate the movies like poison" (38). Yet he also gets "a kick out of imitating them" (38), as he does on several unlikely occasions: after the elevator operator beats him up (136) and after Carl Luce abandons him in the bar (194-95).

His mixed feelings are shown by his remark that the movie at the Radio City Music Hall was "so putrid I couldn't take my eyes off it" (179). He displays similar ambivalence towards other exhibitions: bleeding after Stradlater has beaten him, he finds that the gore "partly scares" and "partly fascinates" him (59); watching the "perverts" in the hotel where he is staying, he observes that "the trouble was, that kind of junk is sort of fascinating to watch, even if you don't want it to be" (87).

His ambiguous feelings about movies and other forms of public exhibitionism are a serious matter, because he had already been invited to appear in a movie short about golfing (100). He refused, because he thought that anybody who hated the movies as he did would be a "phony" if he appeared in one. Was his refusal, however, that simply motivated? He has much to say about the "phoniness" of celebrated performers. He says that if he were a piano player like "Old Ernie" at the night club he visits, he'd "play it in the goddam closet." Ernie's success has made him a snob, so that he doesn't even know "any more when he's playing right or not" (110). Holden has similar objections to the very perfection of the Lunts' acting. "They didn't act like people and they didn't act like actors," he explains. "They acted more like they knew they were celebrities and all. I mean they were good, but they were *too* good" (164). The only public performer who actually pleases him is the drummer at the Radio City Music Hall, who doesn't get to play much, but—when he does—"does it so nice and sweet, with this nervous expression on his face" (179).

Holden's feeling that the Lunts are "too good" and his admiration of the drummer's "nervous expression" show that Holden can identify with the drummer and not with the Lunts because the boy knows that he would be worried about any performance of his own. He could be "good" himself, but he refuses to do any "trick stuff" while dancing, for he hates guys that do "a lot of show-off tricky stuff on the dance floor." This could be modesty, but it could also be stage-fright. Holden has reason to be nervous, for in his present gawky state, he often fluffs major gestures. He has made himself an outcast at school by losing the fencing team's equipment. His defiant shout upon leaving Pencey is spoiled by his falling downstairs after tripping over peanut shells (68). Trying to act sophisticated when greeting the prostitute, he falls over a suitcase (123). He inadvertently blows smoke into the face of the nuns he admires (147). He doesn't know why he even "started all that stuff" about running off with Sally Hayes (134). He gets drunk and breaks the treasured record that he has bought as a gift for Phoebe (199).

These falls are not designed simply to add "comic relief" to the novel. They are exactly what is to be expected of a boy in Holden's physical and emotional condition. He is too disturbed during this time of crisis to have full control over himself.

When he has regained his composure and come to terms with the "phony" world, he may overcome his hatred of those things that entertain people, as he has his hatred of people themselves. And when he achieves better control over his body and feelings, he may prove to be quite a performer himself.

Perhaps it is not at all ironic that the novel ends near Hollywood, for Holden may find—like his brother D. B.—that he is really at home in the movie capital. *The Catcher in the Rye* proves upon close scrutiny to be the story of an ex-would-be-catcher-in-the-rye. It might more appropriately be titled "A Portrait of the Artist as a Very Nervous Young Man." That the novel is about a young man with an artistic bent is not surprising. Artists are likely—whatever subject they choose—to end up contemplating the problems of being an artist. The tracing of Holden's intellectual development, although the least emphasized part of the book, is the most successful; for, while even the good artist—without other training—has no special insight into the problems of physical or emotional growth, the one thing he may know is the problems of becoming an artist.

This analysis by no means exhausts the possibilities of the intricate pattern of *The Catcher in the Rye*, for every episode—probably every sentence—could be shown to play a specific part in completing the overall design. What I have tried to show is that the novel does not need to be interpreted in terms of any outside conventions or traditions. Rather the significance of any detail may be shown to be in some way related to illuminating the physical, emotional, or intellectual crises that the hypersensitive Holden Caulfield passes through during the brief but terrifying period when he begins to discover that he is not a carefree, childish animal, but a unique human being.

V *Holden Abroad*

Although its idiom and situations are characteristically American, *Catcher* has by no means been confined to an American audience. In an age of nuclear terror, adolescents everywhere—despite cultural differences—are perplexed by the same problems.

The novel was published in England within a month after its American release and has been almost as popular there as at home. First issued as a hard bound, it has been included in the paperbound Penguin series, and David Leitch reports that

180,000 copies of the latter·edition were sold in two years.[10] The first British reviewers took the novel even less seriously than most American ones. The *Times Literary Supplement* (September 7, 1951, p. 561) found that "the endless stream of blasphemy and obscenity . . . palls after the first chapter," and R. D. Charques writing in *Spectator* (August 18, 1951, p. 224) expressed the general sentiment when he wrote that "the tale is rather too formless to do quite the sort of thing it was evidently intended to do." One of the most perceptive criticisms to appear on either side of the Atlantic, however, was contributed to *Punch* by R. G. G. Price:

> The weakness of the novel is its sentimentality. The boy is looking for something and the reader is rightly left as doubtful as the boy what it is. It may be a cause, an attitude, a security. The Search, while the basis for some of the greatest of allegories, is also too often an occasion for self-pity and a sensuous enjoyment of failure. . . . I suspect that this sentimentality is in character, that the author has not invented it but approves of it. This may be merely the reaction of a corrupt European, who prefers a soft surface and a hard core.[11]

The formidable task of translating *Catcher's* distinctive idiom has also been undertaken in a dozen countries, mostly in northern Europe, although Salinger's novel was not as rapidly translated into other languages as such other prominent American works as Herman Wouk's *The Caine Mutiny*. Since the title is based upon Holden's misconstruction of a line in an English song lyric, it has given great trouble to translators who have had little success in arriving at literal equivalents. Some of the foreign titles, however, especially the Japanese and the original Dutch (if the words are taken in the sense in which jazz musicians use them) capture the spirit of the book remarkably well.

According to the United Nations Economic and Social Council's annual *Index Translationum*, *Catcher* appeared in three foreign-language editions in 1952, the year after its publication in this country. The Italian translation by Jacopo Darca was called *Vita da Uomo* (A Man's Life); the Japanese translation by Fuoko Hashimoto, *Kikenna Nenrei* (Dangerous Time of Life); and the Norwegian translation by Åke Fen, *Hver Tar Sin —Så Får Vi Andre Ingen* (Every Man for Himself, and the Devil Take the Hindmost).[12] The other Scandinavian nations had their own editions the next year (1953): in Sweden, *Räddaren I Nöden* (The Rescuer in Time of Need), translated by Birgitta Hammar; and in Denmark, *Forbandede Ungdom* (Outcast Youth), translated by Vibeke Schram, who in 1955 was also responsible for the first recorded translation of *Nine Stories*. A French edition also appeared in 1953, *L'Attrape-coeurs* (The Catcher of Hearts), translated by Jean Baptiste Rossi. The next year (1954) a German translation by Irene Muehlon—who has also translated such British celebrities as Churchill, Maugham, and Orwell—appeared in Zurich and Constance, Switzerland, and in Stuttgart, West Germany, bearing the uninformative title *Der Mann im Roggen* (The Man in the Rye). There was also in 1954 a Dutch edition, *Eenzame Zwerftocht* (Lonesome Ramble)—later changed to *Puber* (Puberty)—translated by Henk de Graaff.

The novel entitled *Ani, New York W-khol Ha-Shear* (Myself, New York, and All the Rest) appeared in Israel in 1956 in a translation by Avraham Danieli. In 1958, the first translation in a Communist country—Yugoslavia—was listed by UNESCO. Nikola Krsić's version bore the apparently literal title *Lovac u Zhito*. Donald Fiene has also located later editions in Czechoslovakia (*Kdo Chytá v Zhito*, translated with a literal rendition of the title by Rudolf Pellar and with a critical afterword by Igor Hájek) and Russia (*Nad Propastyu vo rzhi*—"Above the Cliff in the Ryefield," translated by Rita Wright-Kovaleva). Both of these versions first appeared in magazines in 1960. Fiene also reports translations of the work made in 1961 in Finland, Estonia, Argentina, and Poland.

This is not the time or place to attempt a survey of the reception of *Catcher* abroad, but some report of what has happened in West Germany, the non-English-speaking country where the novel has attracted the most critical attention, provides useful insights into the problem of translation and the international reception of contemporary American fiction. German reviewers received the book—which by 1954 was internationally known— even more enthusiastically than English and American. The distinguished novelist Hermann Hesse himself reviewed *Catcher* for *Die Weltwoche* (December 24, 1953) and said: "Whether one reads this novel as the individual history of a temperamental adolescent boy or as a symbol for a whole nation and people, one is led by the author down the beautiful path from unfamiliarity to understanding, from distaste to love. In a problematical world and time, literary art can achieve nothing higher."[13] *Bücher Kommentare* (a quarterly collection of book reviews the much resembles the unfortunately suspended *United States Quarterly Book Review*) carries in its first issue for 1954 another favorable review by Annemarie Weber, who—after succinctly describing the book—compares it to the work of Hesse himself. She writes that, besides Hesse, "none has yet so well described the dangers of this 'bitter age' from the inside. [*The Catcher in the Rye*] is a nerve-wracking appeal not to fail to see the still helpless child behind the often quite unsympathetic mask, an appeal to perceive the dangers which threaten the tendency toward Good and Nobility in the first crisis of life." Miss Weber thinks that this novel, which deals with "a soul capable of very distinguished love," "fits into the picture" of the United States "a new and significant piece."

The German response to *Catcher* is of particular interest since the first scholarly article in a language other than English to be devoted entirely to an explication of the book is Hans Bungert's "Isolation und Kommunikationsversuche des Jugendlichen" (youth's isolation and search for communication) in *Die Neueren Sprachen* (May, 1960).[14] After noting that Salinger takes the place, for post-World War II American youth, of the whole group of novelists who appeared after World I, Bungert explains that Holden's disturbance is "characteristic to a certain extent of his age group," but that general considerations from the teachings of the developmental psychologists provide nothing more than a starting point for the study of the novel, since Holden's personality "sharply cuts him off from his contemporaries."

Bungert also points out that Holden's terrible isolation is "intensified by the time of the action: in the days before Christmas, the holiday of men united by love," and he perceives that Holden "gives up his suicidal intentions without outside help because of his artistic sensitivities." Most of the action, Bungert explains, is devoted to Holden's "search for communication," which is frustrated because "Sally Hayes is too narrow-minded and superficial, Stradlater is too gross and bored, Carl Luce too egocentric and self-seeking." He agrees with American critics that "the high point of the novel" is Holden's achieving "a community of feeling" with Phoebe, which leads him to recognize at last that his "wish for the preservation of the unsullied purity and beauty" of children is "as unfulfillable and just as illusory as a return to his own lost childhood."

Despite this enthusiastic and perceptive German reception, the German-language edition of the novel has not fared well enough to justify the kind of inexpensive paperbound reprint that is as popular there as here. Some of the reasons for this are suggested by my good friend, Hans Ulherr, an English teacher in the secondary schools of Bavaria, who is familiar with American adolescents and their idiom. He comments that just within the first few pages of the translated book, the distinctive flavor is lost when the last word of "David Copperfield *crap*" becomes *Zeug*, meaning just "stuff." "My parents would have about two hemorrhages apiece" becomes "my parents would have fits," and the typically adolescent image, "as cold as a witch's teat" becomes just "as cold as hell." In the typical Caulfieldian expression, "they got a bang out of things, though—in a *half-assed* way, of course," the italicized word becomes "whimsical." Dr. Ulherr explains that "translating 'half-assed' by "*schrullig*" in itself would not be so bad, since it seems next to impossible to find a German equivalent for the original word; but the whole passage in the translation doesn't make much sense when it goes on into the next sentence—'that sounds mean to say,' which is translated literally." The worst blunder in the opening pages, however, is the complete omission, in the description of the head master's daughter, of the phrase "she had on those damn falsies that point all over the place." When the translator comes at last, near the end of the book, to the famous vulgar word that has caused criticism of the original novel, it is indicated simply by the conventional "——."

While the translator, my correspondent continues, expresses Salinger's idea of adolescent tribulation, the German edition "completely fails to convey the hero's language to the German reader" and is, therefore, "not suited to inspire any enthusiasm among the younger generation." No translator, of course, can be blamed for failing to re-create as colloquial a style as Holden's in another language. Since they, unlike the author, are not in a strong enough position to insist upon the integrity of the text, translators must also make concessions to public taste. The point of this discussion is not to criticize the translation so much as to show the basis for Dr. Ulherr's final observation that, after comparing the two versions of *Catcher*, "I am more determined than ever not to read the translation of a book whose original language I can understand.[15]

Very probably the same comments could be made about other translations. The novel was a flop when Robert Laffont first published it in Paris in 1953,[16] and Claude Julien, writing in *Le Monde* on January 13, 1962, still found it necessary to explain to French readers that *Catcher* outclasses several other American novels with adolescent heroes that have attracted nothing like the same kind of response in the United States. Fortunately, the situation in Europe is not so bad as it might be if *Catcher in the Rye* could be known there only in translation, for far more literary-minded German, French, and Scandinavian students read English than American students read their languages. It is very likely, as Bungert implies, that adolescents abroad will become acquainted with Holden in the unadulterated, original form, and that his style of speaking may even flavor their own English.

CHAPTER 9

Feeling Around

I *"Pretty Mouth and Green My Eyes"*

THE VERY WEEK that *The Catcher in the Rye* was published in July, 1951, the *New Yorker* carried Salinger's most sophisticated story, "Pretty Mouth and Green My Eyes," his only attempt to deal exclusively with the problems of mature, professional people already deeply involved in the "ratrace." A feat of technical virtuosity, the story discloses, through the transcription of two telephone calls, the moral collapse of a man completely overwhelmed by the "phony" world.

During his first conversation with a friend who is evidently a member of the same legal firm, the distraught caller confides that his wife has not returned from a party they have all attended. He also discloses that the vain, ambitious woman, whom he calls an "animal," has been playing around with other men and that he has that day lost a case he was trying for the firm. A few minutes later he calls back to report that the wife has returned and to ask the other man to intervene in his behalf with their superior, who will be displeased about the loss of the case. The staggering irony of the situation, however, is that both calls are made to the very man with whom the wife is in bed at the time. The caller has not only been cuckolded, but in his time of distress he is obliged to call upon the very man who is cuckolding him. Small wonder that the deceiver describes the situation as "impossible . . . fantastic."

While the characters are new, this story is closely related to other works of Salinger's. The caller, a man much like Holden Caulfield, is suffering the even worse agony of going through his emotional and professional crisis not during adolescence, but after becoming a supposedly "established" member of society. He even considers briefly—like Holden—simply "running away" from the world of "phonies" by going back into the army, because "at least, it's oblivion." He is too far gone, too deeply committed, however, to escape; for him there is no oblivion, only abject moral disintegration. Denied even the refuge of sticking to the truth by the need to save face, he cannot seek sympathy without deepening his degradation by telling pathetic lies that render him even more contemptible in the eyes of those who are exploiting him.

The wife, like Stradlater in *The Catcher in the Rye*, is a beautiful "animal," who is interested only in "very sexy stuff." She, not Muriel, reserves Seymour Glass's appellation "spiritual tramp," and it is her husband rather than Seymour who has mistaken an impulsive, unprincipled ruthlessness for childish spontaneity. The title of the story comes from a poem that the husband had once written about his wife as he idealized her, but now he realizes that "she doesn't even have green eyes—she has eyes like goddam *sea* shells." (Green eyes also are mentioned in "Uncle Wiggily in Connecticut" and "For Esmé—with Love and Squalor" as attributes of a lovable child.)

The older man is obviously—from his conquest of the wife and his soothing tone on the telephone—a sauve, slick success, like Holden's father, who has adjusted to the "phony" world and fattened on it. Even he, however, is moved by the calls that he receives. When at the end of the story, the girl attempts to help him retrieve a fallen cigarette, he tells her "to just *sit still.*" He may be thinking of his associate's debasement, but he may also—like Eloise at the end of "Uncle Wiggily"—be feeling some lingering regrets about his own fall.

Either Salinger said in this extremely effective story what he had to say about the mature denizens of the "phony" world, or external circumstances—perhaps the disturbing publicity about *Catcher*—caused him to abandon the territory he had just entered, to the disappointment of those who had hoped that he might do for the urban "ratrace" what he had done for prep school life in *Catcher*. "Teddy," his next story for the *New Yorker* (January 31, 1953), was a return to his preoccupation with problem children.

II *"Teddy"*

In "Seymour: An Introduction," Salinger has his "alter ego," Buddy Glass, quote a passage from "Teddy" and comment that it comes from his "exceptionally Haunting, Memorable, unpleasantly controversial, and thoroughly unsuccessful short story about a 'gifted' little boy aboard a transatlantic liner."[1] It is hard to tell from the whimsical context whether or not this is really Salinger's roundabout way of disclaiming the story, but the last two phrases certainly describe it accurately. It is "controversial" and "unsuccessful" because the author does not make clear what actually happens as the story ends with "an all-piercing, sustained scream—clearly coming from a small, female child. It was highly acoustical, as though it were reverberating within four tiled walls." Dismissing as unfathomable and probably irrelevant what "acoustical" could mean in this sentence, the reader is still left uncertain about what has happened to whom. Presumably a ten-year-old boy named Teddy has been pushed into an empty swimming pool by his six-year-old sister; but it is also possible that he has pushed her, or that either of them has jumped or fallen into the pool, or even that the thoroughly nasty little girl is just having a tantrum.

The reason readers are likely to jump to the conclusion that Teddy has been pushed into the pool by his sister is that he has predicted he will be. Children, of course, make lots of dire predictions that mean nothing, but Teddy is no ordinary child. In fact, a large part of the trouble with the story is that he seems to be pure invention. A believer in the "Vedantic theory of reincarnation," he has made some "disturbing predictions" to a religious and philosophical examining group in Boston.[2] As the story opens, Teddy and his family are returning from Europe, where he has performed and made tapes (which have become popular amusements at parties resembling the intellectual gathering at Steiner's in *La Dolce Vita*). Although he denies actually playing fortune teller, he admits to a young educator who grills him that he has told the examiners "places and *times*, when they should be very, very careful." Then, just for instance, he says that when he goes down for his swimming lessons in five minutes, "there might not be any water" in the pool because this might be the day they change it, and his sister might come up and push him in, so that he could fracture his skull and die. Since he has also said earlier in the story—after watching some orange peels sink into the ocean—"After I go out this door, I may only exist in the minds of all my acquaintances," the reader is inclined to believe that the events he has hypothesized may have come true and that it has taken the inquisitive educator just long enough to realize the truth to allow little sister to do her dirty work. The story may simply be a roundabout satire of the sluggishness of the pedagogical mind.

The ending remains controversial, however, because the reader feels that Teddy would not be above simply jumping into the pool and shifting suspicion to the sister who hates him and "everybody in this ocean," or even of pushing her in (possibly "in self-defense"); for Teddy is one of the most obnoxious puppets in the whole history of bratty children. Although he prates about having no emotions, he finds it "rather embarrassing" to hear himself discussed and he gets flustered when the educator addresses him sarcastically. Also, although he scoffs at mere "rational knowledge," he hoards a great deal of it. He asks a female ship's officer the exact time of a "word game" that he assures her is not—as she supposes— over his head. Then he lectures her about the proper way to introduce herself, although it is hard to see why such proprieties would matter to the truly detached soul. He is certainly the kind of person who would know to the minute when the swimming pool is going to be empty.

The reader is also inclined not to take Teddy's word that he is unemotional and nonlogical but to find that he is simply trying to disguise his shrewdly calculating nature. His notebook contains entries about pleasing his father by wearing the man's old army dogtags, avoiding criticism of poets in letters to their husbands, acquiring impressive new words, being nicer to a librarian. Actually at the age of ten, he is bored, cynical, and surfeited with sensation.

Teddy's early satiation with life finally makes the reader feel that what the boy predicted has occurred, for otherwise there seems to be no point to the story at all. Teddy's desire for oblivion is understandable in view of the constant squabbling of his parents—brilliantly dramatized in the opening pages of the story. As Teddy explains to the educator in a remarkable impromptu oration, parents "don't seem to be able to love us just the way we are. They don't seem able to love us unless they can keep changing us a little bit. They love their reasons for loving us almost as much as they love us, and most of the time more. It's not so good, that way." He has also said that he does not predict what will happen, but just times and places where people should be careful. One of these has arrived in his own life. He writes cryptically in his notebook, "It will either happen today or February 14, 1958, when I am sixteen." Since he chooses not to be careful, he, in effect, commits suicide.

One misleading thing about the story is that Teddy's palaver creates the feeling that mysticism is in some way involved in what happens. All Teddy's talk about avoiding "names and emotions," however, is easily explainable as a desperately un-happy child's rationalization for his boredom and frustration. He obviously dislikes being an American (he speaks of being reincarnated in an American body as spiritual retrogression) and even being human (he describes all of the race of Adam addicted to "logic and intellectual stuff" as "apple-eaters.") He would prefer just to be like an elephant, or bird, or one of the trees that attracted Seymour Glass in "A Perfect Day for Bananafish." His longing is an example of the nostalgia for a return to the "uncorrupted" life of uncivilized creatures which colors the party held in *La Dolce Vita* by Steiner (who later kills his children) and which is also exhibited by Holden Caulfield's dream of being a "catcher in the rye." All of Teddy's predictions are explicable, however, as simply the product of a chain of acute logical reasoning. This advocate of unconsciousness is keenly conscious enough to know what people will do under certain circumstances and curious enough to find out when these circumstances will exist. This extremely acute consciousness is what actually causes Teddy's malaise and leads him to seek another incarnation, since he is more sensitive to nuances of speech and behavior than most people.

The story is, thus, a tragedy of wasted sensitivity rendered unaffecting by Teddy's arrogant conceit. Teddy's death—like Seymour's in "A Perfect Day for Bananafish"—seems not so much a gesture of defeat as a desperate exhibition. While such an action on the part of a mature and long-disturbed person like Seymour seems pathetically credible, it seems, when com-mitted by a ten-year-old boy, something staged by the author to drive home a point about adults' insensitivity to "gifted" children which he had already made in many stories without recourse to mystical paraphernalia.

III *"De Daumier-Smith's Blue Period"*

In April, 1953, Salinger collected in *Nine Stories* those of his short stories which he considered worth preserving. All had been previously published in the United States except "De Daumier-Smith's Blue Period," which first appeared in the *World Review* in London in May, 1952. (This magazine also printed "For Esmé" in August, 1950, to introduce Salinger in England.)

In this story, as in some earlier works ("A Girl I Knew," "Blue Melody," for example), Salinger fails to combine the satirically comic and grotesquely tragic material into a whole that has a unified effect. The stories are like paintings in which the backgrounds are not integrated with the important actions in the foreground. Because of the clash of tones in "De Daumier-Smith's Blue Period," the two "epiphanies" that the narrator experiences as he looks into a shop window full of orthopedic appliances are so striking that they distract readers from the rest of the story and are sometimes quoted—by Dan Wakefield, for example[3]—out of the context which gives them meaning.

Ihab Hassan most perceptively criticizes this story when he describes it—like the also awkwardly constructed "The Laughing Man"—as dealing with a character's recollection in manhood of "the guiding revelation of his adolescence." But I think that Hassan is wrong when he says that "De Daumier-Smith discovers that art is less important than the sacramental view of life,"[4] for it is not art but *art training* that the narrator renounces as a result of his experience. As a matter of fact, he adopts the sacramental view of life by consecrating himself to his art. His conclusion that "everybody is a nun" does not mean that all take the same vows.

The story, which concerns a school that teaches painting by correspondence, expounds the same theories of education as "Teddy." Without trying to read these stories as transmuted autobiography, we can recognize that Salinger—in view of his academic difficulties—must have been disappointed with his own education, especially so far as its offering him any preparation to be a writer was concerned. As William Maxwell points out, Salinger "didn't let the curriculum interfere with his self-imposed study of professional writers."[5]

The character who calls himself "De Daumier-Smith" (we never learn his real name) is also disgruntled with his experiences as an art student; yet at nineteen he is willing to take upon himself the job of instructing the correspondence students of an unlicensed art school operated by a Japanese couple in Montreal. Much of the story describes satirically the efforts of untalented students and carries forward the cynically narcissistic tone of the first part, which describes the young man's addiction of self-portraiture.

Among his students, however, De Daumier-Smith discovers a nun who gives evidence of untutored genius. He lavishes his best efforts upon a long letter dictating many instructions to her, asking personal questions about her religious vocation, and pressing her for a personal interview. After he mails it, he has his first "epiphany." Standing before the display window of the orthopedic appliance shop below the art school, he has "forced" upon him the thought that, "no matter how coolly or sensibly or gracefully" he might learn to live, he would "always at best be a visitor in a garden of enamel urinals and bedpans, with a sightless wooden dummy-deity standing by in a marked-down rupture truss."

The next day he receives a letter informing him that the supervisor of the convent school where the nun teaches—a Father Zimmermann, who has the same name as the dentist who removed eight of the young man's teeth—was forced to alter his decision to allow the nun to study through the correspondence school. After reading the letter, De Daumier-Smith writes not only to his other English-speaking students in French telling them that "they were simply wasting their own valuable time as well as the school's but also to Sister Irma offering to undertake her instruction free. If he cannot tutor the genius he has discovered, he will not cater to clods. But he never mails the letter to the nun.

Before he can mail it, he has—accompanied by what sounds like some kind of epileptic seizure—his second "epiphany." Looking in the orthopedic appliance shop window again, he sees a girl in a "green, yellow, and lavender chiffon dress" changing the truss on what he has called "the sightless wooden dummy-deity." When she sees him watching her, he smiles to show his good will, but she becomes flustered and falls over a stack of appliances. When he tries to reach out to her, he succeeds only in hitting the window with his fingertips. His seizure follows. When he recovers, the girl is gone; but she has left behind "a shimmering field of exquisite, twice-blessed enamel flowers." This sight leads him to write in his diary: "I am giving Sister Irma her freedom to follow her own destiny. Everybody is a nun." He also writes to his other students, reinstating them.

Previous discussions of this story have placed emphasis upon the second sentence of the diary entry, but I think the first is more important. As a result of his "epiphany," De Daumier-Smith has identified the girl in the window with Sister Irma; for, to a self-declared agnostic like him, both would seem to be serving "a sightless wooden dummy-deity." When his attention to the girl simply embarrasses her, he realizes that his impulsive gestures of good will toward the nun may have had the same effect. He finds, too, that he cannot really help the girl anyway. When he reaches out to assist her, as he has attempted to reach out to assist the nun, his fingers simply hit the glass.

Out of this experience comes the realization that the art school upstairs is really the same kind of establishment as the orthopedic appliance shop downstairs (even their relative location is symbolic of the parts of man to which they offer help). The only people the shop can help are those who—like his untalented students—need some kind of a crutch. The teacher cannot reach those who are not served by the god, but rather serve him. These people must be left to their own devices, for it is they who turn the "world of bedpans and urinals" into a world of "enamel flowers." When De Daumier-Smith realizes that he cannot help the girl he identifies with the nun, he realizes also that he cannot help the nun either, but must leave her alone to "follow her own destiny." He reinstates his other students, for these he can help; but those with a touch of genius must be left free to learn from their own experience or intuitions. The conclusion that "everybody is a nun" means only that all men live behind walls that others should not violate. We can help only those who ask for help, and these are likely to be the untalented.

Against this theory, we might argue that encouragement may

be invaluable to the struggling novice even if it is occasionally embarrassing. We cannot object, however, to a story's embodying a certain philosophy if it is clearly presented. The objection to "De Daumier-Smith's Blue Period" is to the obscurity of the presentation. Actually the young man's mysterious seizure after his second "epiphany" seems only a rickety dramatic device to give the girl in the window time to disappear; calling the experience "transcendent" (the narrator wisely disclaims that it is mystical) seems simply a distraction device to keep the reader from contemplating the tricky mechanics of the story too closely. The second revelation can be accounted for in entirely rational terms, and the parallel with the first would be clearer if the second were—like the first—just "forced" upon the artist by his talent for making analogies. The experience is "extraordinary" only because the gifted are capable of perceiving unusually subtle analogies.

Even the attribution of the sudden perception to some of neural seizure would add strength to the story by reaffirming the nature of the artist as an especially sensitive sufferer, like whichever of De Daumier-Smith's Japanese employers cries out during the night. While "transcendent" experiences arrest attention, those naturally explicable may be even more awesome and might make more generally significant the change which occurs in a conceited and frivolous young man when he has an experience that gives him an insight into the human capacity for dedicated service. Although the story is not perfectly executed, Salinger does manage to depict in it a man who attains some measure of maturity by learning that he cannot achieve the greatest satisfaction by attempting to impose his ideas upon others.

CHAPTER 10

Search for the Seer

I *Pilgrimage*

IN JANUARY, 1955, I was employed to hold English classes by the University of Kentucky, where "contemporary literature" usually meant the writings of the Nashville "Fugitives" and their offspring, although some iconoclastic students read that upstart Faulkner. I was surprised, therefore, upon returning for the spring semester to find that a story by J. D. Salinger in the previous week's *New Yorker* had disturbed even the tranquillity of this bluegrass fastness as it had rocked more pretentiously in-the-swim academies in the fabled East.

True, much of the initial discussion of "Franny" revolved around a question that has greatly distressed the sensation-hating author, "Is Franny pregnant?" Wise heads nodded yes, and certainly her escort's concern about "testicularity" and the length of time between drinks supported the interpretation that she was; but I just couldn't accept the idea, because if this were simply the story of a girl's guilt feelings during a bout of morning sickness, her nervous hysteria and her escort's overbearing insensitivity were reduced to comic-strip simplicity by the story's erotic overtones. Besides, I could not see why any author would want to diminish the impact of the most telling satire on academic life, in a decade which produced many (Mary McCarthy's *The Grove of Academe* and Randall Jarrell's *Pictures from an Institution,* to mention the strongest competitors), by turning it into another tragedy of what confession magazines might call "youth's careless raptures."

I didn't think then—nor do I now—that we have to read anything into "Franny." Its distinction is that Salinger meticulously lays all his cards on the table. "Franny" is the story he had been trying to tell for a long time about "the last minutes of girlhood." The title character—the youngest of the Glass family, to whom, with this story, Salinger begins to devote himself exclusively—has been having an intense, physical love affair with Lane Coutell, an undergraduate English major at an unidentified Ivy League college.

She has come down to the Yale game, herself gamely determined to try to keep the affair alive; but her infatuation is wearing off. She has written a passionate, childish letter to Lane, but she confesses during lunch. that she had "to strain to write it." She has also quit the theatre to which she has been devoted and has become absorbed in a little book, *Way of a Pilgrim*, that she heard about in a religion course. The book describes the effort of an unidentified Russian peasant to learn how to obey the injunction in St. Paul's First Epistle to the Thessalonians (V, 17) to "pray without ceasing." Although absorbed in an effort to get the "Jesus prayer" described in the book synchronized with her heartbeat so that it becomes practically a part of her personality, Franny has resolved to try to maintain her relationship with Lane. Salinger even points out that if Lane had at one point during lunch returned Franny's smile, the events that followed might have been mitigated, but "Lane was too busy affecting a brand of detachment of his own, and chose not to smile back." The storm breaks.

Franny has already annoyed Lane by comparing him to English department "section men" who "ruin" authors for others by knocking them—who try to build up their own egos by tearing down the distinguished people they present to the students. Lane replies that she has a "goddam bug." After he refuses to return her smile, her attack intensifies: "I'm so sick of pedants and conceited little tearer-downers I could scream." Lane, however, cannot drop an argument until he has won. Acknowledging that there are "incompetent people in all walks of life," he argues that two of Franny's instructors are poets; but she denies even this. They publish poetry, she admits; but instead of leaving behind "something beautiful," they leave only "some kind of terribly fascinating, syntax *droppings*."

Franny is finally prodded into launching forth upon her latest enthusiasm, the *Way of a Pilgrim*. She neglects her meal as she attempts to rouse Lane's interest in this account of the spiritual life, but he is engrossed in eating frogs' legs. Up to this time,

Salinger has relied upon intrusive authorial comments to condition the reader's attitude towards Lane, but he now employs the far more effective device of allowing Lane to break into Franny's joyous account of sharing the pilgrim's adventures with comments showing that he is not touched, interested, or even really listening ("Sounds interesting, you don't want your butter, do you?"). Finally, when Franny runs down, Lane asks, "You actually believe that stuff, or what?". Shortly afterwards Franny faints, and Lane once again does become unselfishly attentive. The point of the fainting is one that Salinger also makes in *The Catcher in the Rye*—people are so preoccupied with their own concerns that they fail to notice that others are getting desperately wrought up until something physically conspicuous happens.

Lane's fault is not really his obsession with a paper he is writing about Flaubert, for his enthusiasm is another example of the kind that Franny feels about her little book. The two young people's behavior differs more in degree than in kind: Lane is self-consciously diffident; Franny is childishly enthusiastic. Just as Holden in *Catcher* exhibits the same "phoniness" he criticizes in others, Franny displays the same absorption in a single idea that upsets her in others. Lane is certainly more like Franny than he is like the "burly-set young man" at the railroad station, "who wanted to know if Lane knew what this bastard Rilke was all about." Lane's shortcoming is not absorption in work but his loving Franny not for herself but for what she does for his ego: before the rupture between them, Lane has "an almost palpable sense of well-being at finding himself . . . in the right place with an unimpeachably right-looking girl." As Franny maintains throughout the conversation, she has given up the stage and has even thought of giving up her major in English because she has become desperately tired of the ego. "I'm sick," she tells Lane, "of everybody that wants to *get* somewhere, do something distinguished and all, be somebody interesting." She wants to be an anonymous pilgrim.

If her romance with Lane is to survive—if infatuation is to become love—she is going to have either to give up her present notions or to convince Lane to share them. All she sees and hears at the restaurant, however—Lane's eagerness to win arguments, to get big *A's*, to get somewhere, and his skepticism of her new enthusiasm—further distresses her. She is finally driven into a pathetic attempt to "convert" Lane ("You might like this book . . . It's so simple, I mean"—hardly the argument to impress a man who is still complimenting himself on his complex analysis of Flaubert). Franny explains what she really wants at this critical stage in her development when she says, "I'm sick of just liking people. I wish to God I could meet somebody I could respect." (Holden Caulfield, too, has been searching for the hero that he never finds, and he himself dreams of being such a hero—"a catcher in the rye"—in the only way the person with no specialized abilities can.) She has liked Lane, as she has liked the "poets" at her school, but she "respects" none of them. This world has failed to provide her with a satisfactory hero; thus at the end of the story we find her "forming soundless words, intoning the prayer to Jesus to have "mercy" upon her—alone in a world of hostile egotists.

Perry Frank, who is as sharp a reader as I know, informs me that "Franny" is incomplete without "Zooey," and she is right. The former story leaves the reader with the question of whether Franny can be brought back into this world or whether she will eventually follow her brother Seymour into oblivion. At the time the story first appeared, no one was disturbed by this incompleteness, because "Franny" was read—at least in the colleges where it became inordinately popular—as an attack upon Lane Coutell. The story did more to establish Salinger's reputation in universities than had *The Catcher in the Rye*, because the "section man" mentality abounds, and many students and even professors—egotistically identifying with Franny—reveled to see it at last get its comeuppance.

In contrast to Miss McCarthy's or Jarrell's novels or even Vladimir Nabokov's delightful *Pnin*, Salinger's story does seem to have been motivated by principle rather than personal spite; and, despite what critics say, there are still people who teach in colleges because they are attempting to maintain principles. Whatever else "Franny" may be, it is one of the most precise and devastating satires to have been written about a world that is full of pedants eager to display their erudition rather than—as one might hope—pilgrims still seeking to learn. The story is still enormously successful as an isolated satire; but Salinger is not content to be a satirist. Considered in connection with "Zooey," "Franny" becomes simply a prologue to an account of the search for individual salvation. "Zooey" appears to have been written to make people see that what matters is not the negative burlesque of the inflated ego, but the positive conquest of it.

II *Redemption*

Between the writing of the two stories, however, something had happened to Salinger. Authors often become depressed or exasperated when readers miss subtle points, just as Lane misses the significance of Franny's increasing excitement. The author may then begin to worry about making his meaning so clear that it cannot be missed or mistaken, and his art begins to suffer—as James Joyce's, for example, never did. For John Steinbeck the turning point came with *The Wayward Bus* and for Faulkner with *Intruder in the Dust* (both written shortly after the end of World War II); it came for Salinger between "Franny" and "Raise High the Roofbeam, Carpenters." By the time he published "Zooey" in the *New Yorker* (May 4, 1957), he was failing to heed the very advice that he had Zooey give his sister, "the stupidity of audiences . . . is none of your business." Despite its tremendously moving conclusion, "Zooey" is a tale in which the author *talks* too much and *shows* too little.

If "Zooey" were altogether what it is in part—the story of Franny's recovery, with her brother's inspired aid, from the breakdown she has suffered in the earlier story—we could unashamedly apply to it the hackneyed and critically unfashionable term "beautiful." Franny's breakdown, whatever else it may involve, has partly resulted from her defeat in a collision of egos with Lane. One reason "Franny" is an unusually well-balanced satire is that Franny's absorption in the Jesus prayer appears as egotistical as Lane's in his Flaubert paper. She is as inattentive to his remarks as he is to hers, although she is sorrier about breaking the spell of his self-enchantment by asking for his olive than he is about breaking hers by asking for her butter. Also, although Franny is angry at "all the conceited little tearer-downers," she does a great deal of tearing down of faculty members and fellow students herself.

All of this is pointed out by her brother Zooey in the story which bears his name. He brusquely reminds Franny that she is pampering herself and that she is not going to "recover" until she becomes absorbed in perfecting herself rather than in condemning others. He tries to get this across to her by pointing out that Christ—"the best, the smartest, the most loving, the least sentimental, the most unimitative master"—is not the sentimental St. Francis that Franny has him confused with. He also tells her that "nobody who's really using his ego, his real ego, has any *time* for any goddam hobbies." He is saying here in a kind of racy, psychoanalytically influenced jargon the same things that William Butler Yeats says near the end of his poem "Among School Children":

> Labor is blossoming or dancing where
> The body is not bruised to pleasure soul,
> Nor beauty born out of its own despair,
> Nor blear-eyed wisdom out of midnight oil.

Both Zooey's and Yeats's statements are professions of a faith that becoming absorbed in a task—living a role—makes one's work and play indistinguishable; but such talk at first only aggravates Franny's condition. When Zooey, however— at first pretending to be his brother Buddy—calls his sister on Seymour's old phone and tells her the now-famous story of the "fat lady"—sitting out in the audience watching the children on the radio —who is really "Christ himself, Buddy," he conveys to her at last what it means to be "God's actress" and not to "rave and bitch" about the stupidity of audiences. "The artist's only concern," he teaches her, "is to shoot for some kind of perfection, and *on his own terms*, not anyone else's." This message absorbed, Franny—like Sergeant X in "For Esmé—with Love and Squalor" and Buddy Glass in "Raise High the Roofbeam, Carpenters"—is able to sleep "as if all of what little or much wisdom there is in the world were suddenly hers."

So far, so good; but, unfortunately, there is much more to "Zooey." The narrator—Buddy Glass—not only has Zooey twice explain to Franny what certainly must be called the "moral" of the story, but he also rubs the reader's nose in it by picturing Zooey, between his own acts, reading a dozen or so quotations from great writers of the past, all of which make the same point he is trying to put across to Franny. Whether Salinger is just working on the Madison Avenue principle that repetition drives a message home or whether he thinks he needs to rally prominent character-witnesses to his support, "Zooey" becomes not so much a unique work of art as a kind of anthology of the wisdom of the past. Zooey even goes to what Salinger has recently been presenting as the highest source of all and reads a passage from what is apparently a diary that Seymour Glass had kept on shirt cardboards.

The invention of Buddy Glass and his "prose home movie" strikes me as Salinger's least felicitous idea, although the "home movie" metaphor is precisely right, because "Zooey," like many home movies, hovers lovingly over those things that mean a great deal to the maker of film and his immediate clique but that simply puzzle and exasperate those who happen to be trapped at a showing. Salinger, of all people, after putting into Holden Caulfield's mouth moving protests against special interest groups banding clannishly together, seems to have become a cultist. As Eliot Fremont-Smith points out, the inaccurate information about his residence that Salinger wrote for the jacket of *Franny and Zooey* is "a joke that insiders . . . can snicker over." The jacket copy thus becomes part of the Salinger-Glass saga, "and the worth of the saga becomes partly determined by one's appraisal of the joke."[1]

Certainly "Zooey"—as most reviewers have agreed—is far too long, because Salinger incorporates into the text—and even into a footnote that he calls an "aesthetic evil"—all of the background material about this beloved, imaginary family that must be in his mind if he is to write of them consistently. But the reader needs to know this only if it is directly relevant to the particular crises around which a story centers or if he and the writer share some extraliterary infatuation, like the "saga" with its private jokes.

How many of the purchasers who have made *Franny and Zooey* a bestseller have read every word of the second story? Many readers who find in the Glass family a sense of community lacking in their own lives do enjoy the long accounts of the family's eccentricities that fill up the opening pages of the story, but such people are likely to grow as impatient with Zooey (and Salinger) as Holden Caulfield does with Antolini when the speechmaking starts. Those, on the other hand, who are reading the stories for the "message" (and surely many reviewers have seized upon it) find the opening pages sluggish. In attempting to provide something for everyone, Salinger fails, I feel, to quite please any except those who now accept undiscriminatingly anything he offers.

Buddy Glass's "home movie," however, needs more than mere judicious cutting to keep the central matter of Franny's recovery from getting lost in the lush background. A more fundamental weakness is that we have no idea whether this recovery is permanent. Since it has, after all, been effected by a talented entertainer, it bears a fishy resemblance to those of a tent revivalist, which may take, but usually don't. We are not sure whether we are reading about the end of a pilgrimage or the upshot of a revival meeting. Is Zooey Glass a cigar-smoking Christ or an ascetic Elmer Gantry?

The permanence of Franny's recovery is especially in doubt since cures do not often last long with the self-indulgent; and, as Eliot Fremont-Smith points out, the world of the Glasses is "the world of the self-indulgent who think they are exceptionally bright when they are only bright . . . in which mannerism is mistaken for charm and problems of morale are rarified into problems of morality." Is this confusion of morale and morality—which leads the Glasses to mistake their vocations with religious callings—simply the character's or is it the author's?

Henry Anatole Grunwald attempts to defend the story from earlier attacks by pointing out that Zooey's views are in character and cannot be unhesitatingly attributed to the author. He sees the story as simply the account of the way in which a gifted actor talks his sensitive sister out of a nervous breakdown. If one accepts this theory, however, the reason for the long introduction acquainting us with the family and its problems and for the host of quotations from the wise men of the past becomes obscure. Grunwald's argument that Salinger approaches his characters ironically would have great merit if "Zooey" were the kind of sparse, single-track narrative that "Franny" is; but the host of details showing the family's weaknesses as well as strengths does not seem to have been introduced at all to pass judgment upon them, but only to make them more real. Salinger is indulgent to his dream-children when he implies to the reader, "See, they're not perfect; they've got lovable human failings." The fact that Salinger apparently expects the reader to surmise that Franny is unambiguously cured indicates the tacit assumption that some kind of pact exists between author and reader. What does the reader who has never heard of Salinger (there may be a few) make of "Zooey"? *The Catcher in the Rye* is the kind of book that attracts us to the author, but "Zooey" is a work to which the author must attract us.

If we do not accept the views expressed in the story as those of the sponsor, the whole thing becomes an astonishingly cynical exploitation of the sentiments of those who still believe somewhat fuzzily, but ardently in the possibility of universal love. Salinger is, of course, famous for his leg-pulls, and even his whole much-publicized "withdrawal" could be designed to keep a thoroughly gulled public from penetrating his cynical mask. If it is, Salinger is one of the most consummate counterfeiters in literary history, one so thoroughly conversant with feelings that he does not share that he is able (as those who employ motivational research would like to be) to exploit the deepest and most troublesome of other peoples' feelings in order to peddle his wares.

If he is such an artist, he should be working on Madison Avenue; and if he has no scruples about exploiting people, it is impossible to see why he isn't. I simply do not believe that the little we do know about Salinger suggests that he is capable of the unnaturally cool detachment that would enable him deliberately to manipulate other peoples' feelings. His slow production and comparatively few successes in creating thoroughly integrated works also suggest that he is not technically a deft enough craftsman to grind out mechanical works that do not mirror his own secret fears and desires. "There are *nice* things in the world," Zooey tells Franny; and I think that Salinger wishes his stories of the Glass family to be among them. They are most completely explicable as his attempt to share with others the *nice* world he has invented as a personal refuge from the *phony* world that threatens to engulf us.

If I find "Zooey" artistically thin, it is not because I feel that the author is simply manipulating words like someone writing a commercial for a deodorant, but—quite the contrary—because I agree with John Updike that in "Zooey," Salinger "robs the reader of the initiative upon which love must be given" and "clinches our suspicion that a lecturer has usurped the writing stand."[2] The longer I contemplate *Franny and Zooey*, the more certain I feel that the public has been right in its enthusiastic reception of the book's general "message" about the advisability of improving one's self rather than criticizing others and that the reviewers have been right in their reservations about the craftsmanship of the presentation. In short, *Franny and Zooey* is not distinguished art, but a self-improvement tract. It belongs on the shelf not beside Scott Fitzgerald, but Emile Coué.

III *Recollection*

After the appearance of *Nine Stories,* Salinger published in almost a decade only four stories, all in the *New Yorker.* The last of these, "Seymour: An Introduction," appeared in June, 1959. In January, 1963, it was collected along with "Raise High the Roofbeam, Carpenters," which had appeared before "Zooey."

Both stories are concerned with the character who has supplanted Holden Caulfield as the central figure in Salinger's writing, Seymour, eldest of the seven Glass children—known for years to audiences of the "It's a Wise Child" radio program as the Blacks. More is known about Seymour, whose life ended in suicide in Florida in March, 1948, than about Salinger himself. Seymour's last moments are described in "A Perfect Day for Bananafish" (1948), the short story that first brought Salinger recognition and that appeared even before the date later assigned to the suicide in Buddy Glass's letter in "Zooey." Seymour's goggles appear fleetingly in "Down at the Dinghy," which also suggests that Buddy Glass's proper name—never later revealed— may be Webb.

Just why Salinger has become obsessed with Seymour is a challenge to readers, who may find the clues in two recent stories about him. These—like "Zooey"— represent a new departure in Salinger's fiction or in almost any fiction since the imitators of *Tristram Shandy* wore out their welcome. Both are a kind of garrulous first-person monologue, filled with confidential asides that acquaint the reader more with the narrator than with his subject. Much so-called criticism of these stories has proved to be simply the critics' outraged reaction to the unusual form, a response understandably provoked by the narrator's air of letting down his hair in public instead of getting on with the show. Before proceeding, I should confess that, like Burling Lowrey, I find at least the last of these stories "a crushing bore," which leaves me "with a feeling of nervous impatience similar to that of being trapped at a bar by a drunk with total recall."[3] Salinger does indeed seem drunk with the fascinated contemplation of his own characters.

Like "Franny" and "Zooey," the two stories about Seymour are related, but not in the sense that the second is a continuation of the first. "Raise High the Roofbeam, Carpenters," in which Seymour appears only in the conversation of others and through some entries from his diary, is designed simply to prepare the audience for the main act. If things must be assigned to genres, this story should be classified with overlong introductions of famous people delivered by those who wish to impress upon the audience how well they know the guest of honor and what a great guy he really is. But in "Seymour," the speaker that we have just listened to announces that since the subject of his encomium killed himself before he had a chance to be heard from, the previous speaker will regale us with detailed recollections of his abilities, appearance, and wisdom.

The scattered criticism of "Raise High the Roofbeam, Carpenters" consists largely of observations that it is a "philosophical dialogue" rather than a short story—although it isn't—and that it somehow sheds light on "A Perfect Day for Bananafish"—although it doesn't. To dispose of the latter charge first, it is difficult to think of a more foolhardy practice in literary criticism than the attempt to interpret an extremely polished traditional short story about a hitherto unmentioned character by a practically unknown author in the light of a long, experimental work published seven years later by an immensely celebrated author who has become obsessed with this same character. In "Seymour," even Salinger himself attempts to warn readers from considering the stories jointly, by having Buddy Glass announce that the man "who did the walking and talking in that early story, not to mention the shooting, was not Seymour at all." But this warning came too late to keep Gwynn and Blotner from speculating that "Raise High the Roofbeam" may be Salinger's compulsive attempt to explain why Seymour killed himself in "A Perfect Day for Bananafish" or to save William Wiegand from flatly stating that the later story "amplifies and explains" the other.

Actually the heroes of the two stories have little in common besides their names. (Why Salinger insists on retaining the same name is another unfathomable mystery, unless he is really obsessed with the notion of a seer named "see-more.") The first Seymour, as I have explained in discussing "A Perfect Day for Bananafish," has a psychotic compulsion to be the center of attention that makes him insult grandmothers, tell tall tales to strange children at the beach, and play the piano in the public rooms of a convention hotel. The second Seymour is so painfully shy that he cannot face being married before a large crowd, and he cannot even find voice to tell his intended that he can't. His greatest problem is that he doesn't "relate to people." He has appeared on a children's radio-quiz program, but "he went down to the broadcast every Wednesday night as though he were going to his own funeral." The first Seymour, on the other hand, brought about his own funeral as the end of his campaign to upset his wife's composure.

While the first Seymour displays an engrossing and colorful imagination in his tale of bananafish, there is no hint that he is the poet of the century; but the tales of the second Seymour are written largely to celebrate his practically unequalled but unrecognized poetic genius. Both men do have troubles with their in-laws and show signs of paranoia, but it is also evident that Salinger had done a lot of daydreaming about Seymour in the years between the writing of the stories. The result is that a quite different and more complex character emerges the second time we meet him.

Actually only the second Seymour is the "bananafish" who commits suicide when he finds himself trapped in a situation from which he cannot escape. Salinger could have had this concept of Seymour in mind when he wrote the first story, but he did not succeed—if that is what he then intended—in successfully paralleling Seymour with the bananafish described in the story within the story. Muriel, Seymour's wife, is even more drastically different in the two stories than Seymour is. The first Muriel is a tough-minded, determined, self-possessed sophisticate, who actually very closely resembles the matron of honor in the second story; the second Muriel is a naïve creature with easily bruised feelings and little discretion, who is much like the first Seymour and whom the second Seymour admires for her lack of discrimination and undeviating love for the institution of marriage. Only Muriel's meddling, psychiatry-conscious mother remains consistent enough to link the two stories in which she is heard but not seen.

The other charge—that "Raise High the Roofbeam, Carpenters" is not a well-constructed short story—is understandable in view of its extreme length and wordiness, but beneath the meandering torrent of words there is discernible the kind of structure that Salinger was not able to break away from completely. He does manage in this story to recount the principal events of Seymour's wedding day: the groom's failure to turn up at the church and his later elopement with the bride from the family apartment. This gentle satire of pretentious social conventions could have been told in a story no longer and no less objective than "A Perfect Day for Bananafish," but "Raise High the Roofbeam" is not really just the story of the wedding day. It is rather the story of a duel over the interpretation of Seymour's character between Edie Burwick, the strong-minded matron of honor, and Buddy Glass, the unassuming brother who is closest to Seymour. As Buddy confesses at the beginning of the story, using a Taoist tale about the best judge of horses, he has not since Seymour's death been able "to think of anybody whom I'd care to send out to look for horses in his stead." When Seymour fails to appear for his nuptials, Buddy is obliged to defend his opinion against the charges which the matron of honor sums up in her question, "Does that sound like a normal person—a normal man . . .? Or does it sound like somebody that's either never *grown up* or is just an absolute raving maniac of some crazy kind?"

Feeling outnumbered as long as he—just an army enlisted man —is riding in a closed car with the matron, her officer husband, Muriel's aunt, and Muriel's father's tiny deaf-and-dumb uncle, Buddy holds his tongue and tries to keep from identifying himself until—through an unlikely chain of events—he shepherds the group to his and Seymour's old apartment for drinks. Then finally goaded beyond endurance by the matron's assertion that Muriel's mother has said Seymour is "absolutely unfit for marriage," Buddy breaks in with a speech, which he later feels may be "the stuff that heart attacks are made of." He says that "from the time Seymour was ten years old, every *summa-cum-laude* Thinker and intellectual men's-room attendant in the country had been having a go at him," but that not one of "all the patronizing, fourth-rate critics and column writers, had ever seen him for what he really was. A poet, for God's sake." Buddy goes on to shout that even if Seymour "never wrote a line of poetry, he could still flash what he had at you with the back of his ear if he wanted to." No argument ensues, for a dramatically convenient distraction occurs. Buddy's championing of Seymour is finally vindicated, however, by the marriages coming off all right. After it does, Buddy is able—like the Sergeant in "For Esmé"—to drop off to sleep.

The story cannot be dismissed, however, with an analysis of its slender structure; for it does pose a "philosophical question"—Does Seymour's doing right by Muriel vindicate Buddy's description of him as a poet? The concept of a poet who may never write a line occasions, of course, the Taoist fable about the best judge of horses entirely ignoring externals, because Buddy Glass determines people's vocations by their internal qualities alone. But in order to grant that Seymour really differs from the erring wife in "Pretty Mouth and Green My Eyes," who fancies herself "the greatest living undeveloped novelist," we must accept Buddy Glass as a good judge of horses—not just a man showing fraternal partiality. The effort to make the reader think more highly of Buddy than of the "intellectual men's room attendants" accounts for the length of the story and the details chosen for inclusion. "Raise High the Roofbeam, Carpenters" is actually what textbooks would call a "character sketch." Its purpose is not so much to tell a story as to present a "memorable" character in a favorable light. The character sketched, however, is not Seymour, but Buddy. If the reader responds properly to Buddy, he will then accept and share Buddy's opinion of Seymour.

The story does not really convince at least this critic, however, that Buddy does a very good job of objectively classifying someone as close to him as Seymour has been; and, if any of Buddy's classifications are questionable, so is his designation of Seymour as a poet. Buddy's judgment can be challenged on the basis of his statement that Seymour isn't an "exhibitionist," because back in the days when the boys were on the radio, Seymour "didn't even talk to you . . . the whole way down on the bus or subway." Buddy fails to consider that one may be an exhibitionist only while on stage and that Seymour could simply be concentrating beforehand on ways to improve his performance. Dramatic silence may also be an extreme form of exhibitionism in itself.

Certainly traces of the first Seymour—who was a pathological exhibitionist—are discernible in the second Seymour when it is reported that he said Lincoln at Gettysburg should simply have shaken his fist at the crowd, and especially that he once threw a rock and seriously harmed a girl named Charlotte who was on the radio with him and who has since become a movie star. This violent behavior is one of the principal evidences the matron of honor offers of Seymour's abnormality. Asked if the story is true, Buddy says "yes," but he never gives his explanation for Seymour's behavior until he is left alone with the mute uncle. Then he announces that, although the girl herself never understood why Seymour threw the rock, everybody "in the family" knew that is was because "she looked so beautiful sitting there." Even if we question the matron of honor's charge that the episode shows that Seymour is a "raving maniac," we may wonder if his family is not simply trying to rationalize Seymour's violent jealously of the girl's beauty, personality, or talent. In explaining away the episode, the family here seems to be exhibiting the reverse of the trait that Eliot Fremont-Smith comments upon and to be passing off a matter of morality as a matter of morale. Actually it could be violent jealousy rather than excitement that makes Seymour wish not to share his wedding day with a crowd of his bride's relatives. Seymour may even have developed the notion that he is "a kind of paranoiac in reverse"—one who suspects people of "plotting" to make him "happy"—because of the uncritical affection of a family who has rationalized his misbehavior and has indeed plotted to make him happy.

The story may give an insight into Salinger's curious notion of what family life should be like, for it would seemingly be difficult to write approvingly of a self-admiring family like the Glasses without approving of them. The conservatism, the affection for siblings, the plea for undiscriminating love that underlie so much of Salinger's work could result from a basic notion that that family circle is the place where the individual need not be "understood" at all; he should simply be exempted from criticism. (The same notion underlies the gripes against parents trying to change children in "Teddy".) While such a family attitude would certainly provide security for the sensitive individual, it would also render him just as ill-prepared to "relate to other people" as Seymour is reputed to be. The rock that Seymour threw at Charlotte may be one example of how his family relationships left him ill-prepared to deal with other problems of life. Certainly Buddy's indulgent explanation of the incident undermines our faith in his ability to evaluate the family impartially.

Apparently the blow did break up the affectionate relationship between Charlotte and Seymour, although this relationship may have left an impression upon him (as well as her). According to his diary, Seymour is marrying Muriel because he needs her "undiscriminating love." Muriel's aunt suggests another explanation, however, when she examines a photograph of Charlotte as a youngster and points out that Muriel—whom Buddy has not seen—looks exactly like her. With the introduction of this detail about the resemblance between Charlotte and Muriel, many of the "arrangements" that Salinger had to contrive for the story fall into line—Seymour's family's lack of acquaintance with Muriel; Seymour's fascination for the naïve and unimaginative Muriel, which he rationalizes at such length in his diary; Seymour's fear of "being too happy," which might provoke him to behave irresponsibly; and Buddy's maneuvering this particular group of characters into an apartment that contains a childhood picture of Charlotte.

If Seymour is marrying Muriel in an effort to recapture his lost childhood sweetheart, there is surely something to the matron of honor's charge that he has "never grown up." Another evidence of his immaturity is that, although he keeps an extensive diary, he rarely writes letters—even to his indulgent family. Actually this "precocious" child who entered Columbia at fifteen seems never to have matured emotionally, and it is very likely that this persistence of childish feelings in an adult with a superior intellect makes practical-minded people like the matron of honor denounce him as a maniac and at the same time enables Buddy to consider him a poet. Seymour, however, does not really deserve either title. The matron's judgment is unduly harsh, but Buddy's is overly indulgent and sentimental (jealous impetuosity is a childish characteristic that is likely to be interpreted as either madness or artistic talent only by the undiscriminating).

If, in his impassioned speech, Buddy had simply defended Seymour's honor, the outcome of the day's events would have vindicated his faith and the story would have been a defense of the eccentric person of integrity against a convention-ridden world eager to make people adjust. Salinger, however, is not Sinclair Lewis. In the speech he assigns Buddy, Salinger attempts to make the reader believe that a poet says and does what he really believes. But what about others? Unless the statement can be converted to read that the only person who says and does what he believes is the poet, all we can be sure of is that Seymour and poets have a common characteristic. Buddy's statement, however, cannot be validly converted, and the syllogism he employs to make Seymour a poet is faulty.

The result is that "Raise High the Roofbeam, Carpenters" degenerates into a special pleading that must be accepted on faith, and one should be careful about accepting uncritically the pronouncements of those who claim that their own kind (Salinger, after all, is himself an artist) are the only men of integrity. The very story line, however, that necessitates the introduction of Charlotte into "Raise High the Roofbeam, Carpenters" to explain Seymour's seemingly inappropriate choice of a wife also necessitates providing the reader with enough evidence so that he may reach some conclusions of his own that differ from the narrator's. Possibly it was the desire to exercise even more complete control in shaping the reader's thought that led Salinger in devising "Seymour: An Introduction" to abandon objective storytelling altogether and to write unabashed propaganda.

IV *Resurrection*

Henry Anatole Grunwald remarks that "Seymour" is "a story remarkably little discussed by critics, and, one may guess, widely misunderstood." It has been, however, frequently and often unfavorably discussed, and it is easier to understand than many stories in which the meaning is concealed in a dramatic metaphor. Grunwald's own explanation of the story is an apt analogy with the work of playwrights like Pirandello and Jack Gelber who are "trying to destroy the proscenium" and "bring the audience completely into the action, to make them forget what is real and what is not." Few critics would disagree, but they might still ask, "To what end?" One who goes around destroying prosceniums to no purpose is a vandal. Why does Salinger deliberately, by assigning his own stories and rumors about himself to his narrator, attempt to confuse the two? The only reason for breaking down the aesthetic distance between writer and reader is that the writer wishes to establish the kind of rapport that will make the reader share the narrator's feelings. Literature becomes not a comment upon experience, but an experience in itself for those in want of other experiences. The question about a work like "Seymour" (leaving aside the important problem of the artistic stature of a work that supplants rather than illuminates other experience) is what kind of experience does it offer?

The "Introduction" falls into five unequal parts. The first, which Buddy calls a "credo," is a long, genial chat with the "general reader," setting him and the narrator apart from Beatniks and other cultists and advising those not interested in exciting flights of the imagination to stop reading. (For those who have business of their own, this is good advice.) In this introduction, Buddy prepares for the second part by asking, as "Raise High the Roofbeam, Carpenters" would lead us to expect, if the "true poet or painter" isn't actually "the only seer we have on earth?" The long second section then introduces Seymour as seer—a poet who will eventually stand with "only three or four *very* nearly non-expendable" ones we have had. We are offered no evidence of this genius' skill except a verse written when he was eight and prose paraphrases of the two final poems in the collection that Buddy is supposed to publish some day. Probably Salinger did not have the temerity to put forward verse that he thought would exhibit the qualities he attributed to Seymour. He was in the same position as the novelist who cannot provide illustrations of his characters' reputedly scintillating conversation. The paraphrases that are offered, however, confirm suspicions that Seymour's poems are "cute" renditions of scenes that are tremendously meaningful only to the writer. The only other evidence provided of Seymour's "seermanship" is an anecdote concerning his ability at the age of eight—without asking questions—to bring all of the unfamiliar guests at a large party their proper hats and coats. The very brief third section illustrates Seymour's not especially distinctive qualities as a prose stylist in some morale-boosting but nonspecific criticisms of Buddy's stories.

The seemingly interminable fourth section is a physical description of Seymour, whom Buddy seems to be describing more to himself than to the reader. The passage is reminiscent of the long descriptions of people and places that Sinclair Lewis used to write to provide himself with background for his novels, but which he usually had the discretion to spare the reader. Finally the real meat of the story comes in the fifth section in which Buddy—after this enormous build-up—reverts to something approximating traditional short-story form to explain some of Seymour's endearing characteristics. In point of fact Salinger buffs will find little that is new in this last section. *Seymour* exhibits precisely the qualities that any follower of Salinger's previous fiction might predict: an indifference to clothes and other materialisms, an ability to do without sleep nights on end when absorbed in a problem, a distaste for "winning"—especially from people he liked. The end of the story almost exactly duplicates the "fat lady" speech at the end of "Zooey." Thinking about his forthcoming college class, Buddy Glass meditates: "There isn't one girl in there, including the terrible Miss Zabel, who is not as much my sister as Boo Boo and Franny. . . . Seymour once said that all we do our whole lives is go from one little piece of Holy Ground to the next. Is he *never* wrong?"

The "lurid" question about Seymour's suicide that might intrigue many readers is answered quite early in the story, so that those interested only in sensations need go no further. Buddy explains: "The true artist-seer . . . is mainly dazzled to death by his own scruples, the blinding shapes and colors of his own sacred human conscience." While this answer is far from self-explanatory, William Wiegand is apparently quite right about the Seymour of the later stories being "glutted with sensation."

So back to the question of the destruction of the proscenium. What kind of experience does the story offer? The experience, of course, of knowing Seymour. Salinger is infatuated with the character, and he would like us to be, too—to think of him, in fact, not as a character, but as a real man. Hence, the ax to the proscenium.

The reason for Salinger's infatuation is apparent from the already quoted description of the true poet as our "only seer." "Seymour" is the attempt to acquaint us with this seer. The story is actually not a description of Seymour—which would render him too patently fictional—but a description of a writer (who has actually written stories signed with the name that appears at the end of this story) trying to recall what to include in a description of Seymour that he is writing. Salinger deliberately keeps introducing side comments from Buddy to the reader and even to himself to remind us that he is not so much conjuring up a fictitious Seymour as creating a picture of another writer—who does not share the author's history but who is said to have written his stories—recalling a Seymour who has been quite real to him. The many comments about how the act of recollecting Seymour helps Buddy to sleep show the salutary effect on a less-privileged mortal of contemplating a seer.

In fact, the aim seems to be to let less-privileged mortals "in" on something of the nature of the creative act itself. It is an effort to provide those who find their lives drab and monotonous with something more colorful. The temptation to search for autobiographical elements in such a work is great, but it should be resisted. Several comments on autobiographical elements in literature within "Seymour" suggest why an attempt to identify episodes of the story with events of Salinger's life will lead us away from the point of the narrative rather than towards it. Buddy observes first that "the more personal Seymour's poems appear to be, or *are*, the less revealing the content is of any known details of his actual daily life in this Western world." Later he adds that, although Seymour's poems "couldn't be more personal, or reveal him more completely, he goes through every one of them . . . without spilling a single really autobiographical bean."

An artist could not, of course, possibly exclude all autobiographical material from his work, but hunting for this material is likely to distract us from the repeated distinction Salinger makes between *autobiographical* art and *personal* art—the first is drawn from his real life; the second, from the life he imagines he would like to lead. Just as *The Catcher in the Rye* is the culmination of Salinger's contemplation of the "phony" world in which we live, so his stories of the Glass family are his vision of the "nice" world in which he would like us to live. He is in this "nice" world when he is with the Glasses, just as many other people are in their "nice" world only during the time they spend with a more literal glass in their hand. It is not at all unfair to say that the stories of the Glass family are literary moonshine. Nor should we wonder that Salinger has Buddy Glass vigorously disclaim any connection between Holden Caulfield, who is all too clearly immured in the "phony" world, and Seymour Glass, who in his second manifestation is the personification of the author's ideals.[4]

But why this worship of Seymour? I have pointed out that *The Catcher in the Rye* is the work of a conservative who is not interested in overthrowing existing institutions but in providing a decent world for sensitive youths who are not strong-willed enough to flaunt tradition. The novel is the tale of such a boy's coming reluctantly and painfully to terms with his society. "Raise High the Roofbeam, Carpenters" implies, as we have seen, that the family should provide the individual with an uncritically affectionate response. It would not be at all surprising if, as *Newsweek* reports, Salinger is a registered Republican.[5] He would favor a party that avowedly supported stability. Such satirical protests as he makes are against those who threaten the tranquillity and order of the world in order to "get somewhere." It is especially noticeable that none of Salinger's central characters ever have financial problems that cause them discomfort.

Yet Salinger has been fascinated—as James Thurber's "The Secret Life of Walter Mitty" brilliantly suggests the timorous often are—with the vision of the man who allows himself to be destroyed rather than to compromise with phoniness. Many such figures might be imagined; but as Salinger's reaction to Hemingway and the Beatniks shows, he resents those who actually thumb their noses at bourgeois proprieties. Nor can he accept dynamic world-shakers who are too strongly motivated by materialist goals. To satisfy him, the holdout must share Holden Caulfield's sense of universal compassion. He must, in short, be a man with an extraordinary capacity to "get somewhere" who then chooses not to use it. Since life provides few such paragons, Seymour is created.

Holden Caulfield and Seymour Glass are similar in that they both honor the commandment to love one's neighbor as one's self; there is, however, a significant difference between them. Holden, who is appallingly human, is weak enough to compromise at last rather than run too great a risk of destroying himself or those he loves; Seymour—as he emerges in the later stories—is a kind of emotional superman who has risen so far above self as to destroy himself rather than either compromise with society or destroy others (actually he appears to remain too childish to compromise). He is the result of Salinger's preoccupation with the question of how to admire a suicide. He find the answer in Buddy's statement that the artist is "dazzled to death by his own scruples." The man who can compromise will never know such dazzling brilliance. This is why Salinger has Buddy say of Seymour, "I'm writing about the only person I've ever known whom, on my own terms, I considered really large." If we substitute "created" for "known"—as is justified by the relationship that Salinger has established between himself and his "alter ego"—we understand the motive of the stories about Seymour.

The value of the experience that Salinger thus offers the reader is a matter that the individual must decide for himself. I have some quarrels with Salinger's point of view, but I reserve these for the conclusion of this book. My reason for considering "Seymour: An Introduction" a "crashing bore" is that I do not think it is a serious work of art at all. Serious art, I believe, helps us to understand our experience, assists us in coming to terms with it, but it does not replace it. Works of fiction that seek to replace rather than illuminate our experience are *kitsch*, which I think is best defined as that which describes feelings no one actually feels. *The Catcher in the Rye* is serious art; "Seymour: An Introduction" is self-indulgent *kitsch*.

CHAPTER *11*

A Dora Copperfield Kind of Complex

I HAVE BEFORE ME a pamphlet circulated by "The Committee to Oppose the Canonization of Karl Marx, Miami, Florida." Its title asks the frightening question, "Are Your Children Being *Brainwashed* in Dade County Public Schools?" The Committee's answer, of course, is "Yes." The inner of the four-pages carry an attack upon Robert Heilbroner's *The Worldly Philosophers* for doing the brainwashing. The back page is devoted to excerpts from *The Catcher in the Rye.*

The pamphlet does not attempt to link Salinger with Karl Marx; rather the quotations from the novel are prefaced only by the statement, "this filth is being recommended to your children for extra-curricular reading. . . . Is this the kind of book that should be recommended reading by teachers in our public schools?" Presumably *Catcher* is under fire because such "filth" can so deprave guileless schoolchildren that they are softened up for Marxist indoctrination.

Salinger has been attacked before by self-appointed censors. A Houston lawyer stirred up a debate in the newspapers when he withdrew his daughter from the University of Texas rather than permit her to remain in a class where the novel was used. Mrs. Beatrice Levin found herself a community issue when she recommended *Catcher* to her high school English students in Tulsa, Oklahoma. Donald Fiene, who himself was dismissed from Louisville, Kentucky's Male High School for reading *Catcher* with a class, has described in *The Realist* a distressing number of attacks upon the novel and actual bannings both in this country and abroad.[1]

Such treatment of *Catcher* is what Holden Caulfield would call "depressing." I am not concerned at the moment with the general issue of censorship; I am opposed to the censoring of artistic materials by unqualified persons—especially religious and governmental groups. But I do not wish to be diverted

[161]

into the vast question of what constitutes qualification. What particularly disturbs me is that the kind of person who attacks Salinger doesn't recognize an ally when he sees one. Far from being a radical attack upon our system that might serve Marxist ends, *Catcher* is written from a conservative viewpoint and is one of the best defenses that we have against the brainwashing of our children. It cannot satisfy, of course, fanatics at either end of the spectrum, for it neither exalts the status quo nor calls for its overthrow. Its argument is essentially that the world is generally "phony," but that it must be accepted as it is by individuals who must work out their own salvation. What Salinger really attacks are parents and educators who try to force youth to accept their own theories while failing to provide the kind of affectionate atmosphere in which children can work out solutions to their own problems.

Edward Corbett, in the weekly Jesuit magazine *America,* examines the repeated charges against *Catcher*: that its language is "crude, profane, obscene," that some episodes are "scandalous," and that Holden while "contantly protesting against phoniness is a phony himself."[2] Corbett goes on to express the opinion, however, that the real reason this one novel that postwar young people avidly read and discuss upsets the older generation so much is that "it exposes so much of what is meretricious in our way of life."

Even this level-headed defense does not explain the real effect that reading the novel is likely to have upon those young people who are susceptible to artistic influences. Those who decry the novel fear that, like some inflammatory documents of the past, it seeks to incite youth to overthrow the social order or to flee from the world they know. They suppose that Salinger is saying—like Mark Twain, for example, at the end of *Huck Finn*—"You can't go home again"; but instead he is saying, "You can't get away." Hugh MacLean hit the mark exactly when he described *Catcher* as "a conservative *No Exit*."[3]

As Ernest Jones's review in *Nation* stresses, the novel records "what every sensitive 16-year-old since Rousseau has felt." While I think that such feelings were felt long before Rousseau publicized them, there is no doubt that the enormous vogue of the novel is the result of its description in the most appropriate language of the disturbed feelings of many American adolescents. Is it, therefore, not likely to incite them to imitate Holden's flight? I think not. At the beginning of the twenty-fifth chapter in which the climaxes of Holden's several crises occur, we find evidence of the viewpoint from which the boy addresses the reader: after relating that he slept on a bench in the waiting room in Grand Central Station, he says, "Don't ever try it. I mean it. It'll depress you" (p. 252). Holden has hoped, by leaving school early, to get "rested up" in New York after his frustrating experiences. Many students are similarly tempted to run away because of conflicts with their associates and failures in their work. When Holden runs away, however, he finds not peace but only more intense forms of the same kind of problems and frustrations he has already experienced.

Other frustrated youths can indulge their fantasy of running away by following Holden's adventures; but, if they do identify with him, they learn that running away solves nothing. Indeed they learn before they start out for themselves that they will accomplish nothing. The point of *Catcher* is similar to that of conservative Samuel Johnson's *Rasselas*, which as Wayne Booth points out, is that there is no sense in participating in the quest described since it is fruitless.[4] The tendency of *Catcher* is thus to discourage a frustrated youth's hope that he may improve his situation by flight. Of all the analysts of the novel, Kingsley Widmer comes closest to assessing its actual effect when he says in "The American Road" that Holden does not "break into freedom" but rather "ritualistically *plays* at the big-boy's kind of freedom just to neutralize and dispel it for easier adjustment." As Widmer further points out, if Holden learns "to love the pervasive phoniness of modern life"—as he does in his last statement about "missing everybody"—"the road and revolt won't be necessary."[5]

The novel is thus not aimed at promoting revolt but at discouraging it—and at encouraging a reconciliation with others who suffer under the burden of man's imperfections. An undergraduate writer, Marc Rosenberg, points out that *Catcher* is not a sweeping indictment of society, since upon finishing it the reader is "not sure how much of the blame for Holden's tragedy should be borne by society and how much by Holden himself."[6] Thus the answers to the objections that Corbett lists as having been posed to the novel are—in reverse order: (1) It is essential that Holden share the world's phoniness if he is to be reconciled to the world—neither Holden nor society is all one might hope, but both are alike; (2) If the situations are scandalous, it is because—as we need only consult a newspaper to discover—the world to which one must adjust is full of comparable situations and adjustment is not facilitated by hiding the truth from the young; (3) Obscene language is introduced only so that Holden can attempt to erase it. He finds the words written in public places. If young children see them, they ask about them and probably get what Holden calls a "cockeyed" explanation from some "dirty kid." Is it better that children thus come upon such words unsuspectingly or that they meet with them in a book where a figure with whom they can identify and sympathize rails against them? I suspect that the reason *Catcher* enrages many who actually teach similar doctrines is that Salinger has been much more successful than they have been in winning the attention and admiration of youth.

The people who actually have a complaint against *Catcher* are those who believe that it is possible to improve the world by conscious, thoughtful effort and who would prefer to see youth identify with a more dynamic, self-possessed hero than Holden. One such complaint was made by a student who told Granville Hicks that "Holden Caulfield's rebellion was too imitative and ineffectual to be worth serious consideration" (Grunwald, *Salinger,* p. 194). I must object that Holden's revolt must certainly be seriously considered simply because so many young people in our society identify their sentiments with his. Salinger presents through a fictional metaphor the challenging argument that Paul Goodman does in *Growing Up Absurd* when he states that "our society is at present simply deficient in many of the most elementary objective opportunities and worth-while goals that could make growing up possible."[7] I agree with Hicks's student, however, that if there is any hope for the regeneration of our society it lies not with the Holdens who do not have the strength to oppose convention (nor the Seymour Glasses who cut themselves off from it), but in those with the strength and self-assurance to talk back to elders who have scuttled principle to court popularity. Such self-possessed young people may achieve what David Riesman calls "autonomy."

Salinger does not appear to believe that the individual can be strong enough to become autonomous without paying a heavy price. He has, through his recent portraits of Seymour Glass, endorsed a kind of nonconformity; but the implication of Seymour's maladjustment and ultimate suicide is that self-assertive behavior imposes a greater strain upon the individual than he can stand for very long. Seymour appears to be the type of person that Riesman would call "anomic" (incapable of conforming to the behavioral norms of his society) rather than "autonomous" ("free to choose whether to conform or not").[8] Salinger, despite his distaste for Beatniks, seems to share their inability to distinguish between unconventionality and genius.

As I have already pointed out in my discussion of Salinger's distinction between the "nice" and "phony" worlds, he seems to doubt Riesman's assertion that "the individual is capable of more than society usually asks of him." Near the beginning of *Catcher*, when Holden's old history teacher says that "life *is* a game when one plays according to the rules," Holden inwardly scoffs: "If you get on the side where all the hot-shots are, then it's a game all right. . . . But if you get on the *other* side . . . then what's a game about it?" (12). Holden has trouble "applying" himself at school because the schools are operated to train the kind of "hot-shots" that society values. They teach one to make good in the conventional manner, but they only frustrate those who seek to be different from the crowd.

Fears, similar to Salinger's, that the schooling demanded by society will crush unconventionality (which may or may not prove to be genius) because the sensitive individual is not strong enough to resist the system have often led to the kind of "back-to-nature" thinking manifested in *La Dolce Vita* and scores of less spectacular entertainments. Salinger flirts with this kind of thinking in "A Perfect Day for Bananafish" and in the "catcher-in-the-rye" speech in his novel; but he is himself too thoroughly imbued with the values of the urban middle class not to find such escapist notions illusory. What he really pleads for in his writing—as Paul Goodman does in *Growing Up Absurd*—is a system of education that is more responsive to the needs of troubled city children and will provide them with a set of values that seem worth striving for. The enormous response to Salinger's work suggests that there must be something generally wrong with our educational system, which can indeed only reflect our generally confused values. In drawing for his writings upon his own unhappy educational experiences, Salinger has struck a note to which many in our society can respond.

I can only admire this argument and Salinger's artistic presentation of it. What distresses me about Salinger is that, having struck back in *Catcher* at the tormentors of adolescents, he has not moved on—as he seemed to be doing in "Pretty Mouth and Green My Eyes" and "Franny"—to expose those who make our adult society such a shabby spectacle. His more recent work does not seem to me to deal with reality at all, but to be an exaltation of the charms of an imaginary childhood.

The children in *Catcher* and *Nine Stories* are not sentimentalized, for they have both engaging and deplorable qualities; and a central issue in two of Salinger's best stories—"Down at the Dinghy" and "For Esmé"—as well as in those scenes near the end of *Catcher* in which Holden tries to get Phoebe to change her mind about running away with him, is how· to help impetuous young animals develop into decent human beings without resorting to repressive tactics that will destroy their spirits. Recently, however, especially in two passages in "Raise High the Roofbeam, Carpenters," Salinger presents children in an almost nauseatingly sentimental manner.

One of these is a diary entry that Seymour bases on the Vedanta: "Raise . . . children honorably, lovingly, and with detachment. A child is a guest in the house, to be loved and respected—never possessed, since he belongs to God." The first sentence soundly summarizes Salinger's educational theories, but the second sums up the story's basic implication that children should not be judiciously criticized but exempted from criticism. It sounds especially syrupy when read in connection with Buddy's explanation that Seymour turned a question-and-answer radio program on which the Glass children appeared into "a kind of children's round-table discussion." The very idea of such a program is grotesque. It is one thing to treat children with respect and detachment, but it is quite another to exalt their cute sayings and belligerent prejudices into a kind of Edenite wisdom.

Of course, it can be argued that in these passages Salinger is not speaking. Even if Salinger had not, however, identified himself with Buddy Glass, the idea of a "child's round-table discussion" being broadcast nationally is so bizarre that I do not see how he could have conceived of it if it did not intrigue him, or mention it unsatirically if it did not please him. As the dedication to *Franny and Zooey* also shows, Salinger is spellbound by the kind of petulant cuteness that Dickens personified in childish Dora Copperfield, whose undiscriminating love finally proved less satisfying to David than Agnes' mature affection. Alfred Kazin writes in his review of *Franny and Zooey* that he is sorry "to have to use the word 'cute' in respect to Salinger, but there is absolutely no other word that . . . so accurately typifies the self-conscious charm and prankishness of his own writing" (Grunwald, *Salinger*, p. 49). The great defect of Salinger's work is that when he tries to summon up the "nice" world he dreams of, he can only create something "cute." He can envision life with Dora, but not with Agnes. There is no picture anywhere in his work of a couple that has been long and happily married, except a few undeveloped paragraphs in "A Young Girl in 1941 with No Waist At All." The Glass parents have been long married, but the father is never depicted.

Undoubtedly part of the reason why Salinger is attracted to "cuteness" is that it is a characteristic of those who are intellectually precocious without having developed sexually. The "sexlessness" of Salinger's world has often been noticed. Although prostitutes, adulterers, and such creatures occasionally darken his pages, they are consistently denounced. His attitude toward sex appears the product, however, not so much of a fear or hatred of sex *in itself*, as of a detestation of *sexual promiscuity*. This hatred extends, furthermore, to any other form of promiscuous behavior, as "Pretty Mouth and Green My Eyes" especially demonstrates. Holden's problem in *Catcher* is not that he rejects sex altogether, but that he is torn between giving into promiscuity—which in all its forms characterizes the "phony" adult world—and trying to hold on to his own "nice" ideals. Salinger's heroes' struggles to hold on to their Victorian ideals account, I think, for their often preferring the company of female children to that of women of their own age. I do not think that Salinger intends any hint in their behavior of the kind of lustful cravings that prompt Humbert Humbert's interest in *Lolita*. Rather, to stay "nice," they must seek out those still too young to feel sexual stirrings, whom they can dream of protecting from becoming contaminated. When older people, however, mingle too long with pre-pubescent children, they are likely to become "cute" themselves.

This idealization of childhood has been called "Peter Panism" but we should be aware that Sir James Barrie does not share his fantastic character's views. Although Peter himself says, "I just want always to be a little boy and to have fun" and "I don't want to go to school and learn solemn things," he does not speak for his creator, who in his last stage direction writes—after Peter refuses to let Wendy embrace him—"If he could get the hang of the thing his cry might become 'To live would be an awfully big adventure!' but he can never quite get the hang of it." "Living" is not an awfully big adventure to Salinger's people.

A possible reason for this preoccupation with childhood is that—as Eliot Fremont-Smith points out—Salinger deals with a world in which *morale* is confused with *morality*. Children's problems are all problems of morale, as they have not yet developed any sense of morality. Indeed the real horror of growing up is that we are forced either to accept or develop moral codes that sometimes oblige us to make uncomfortable decisions or else to drift about aimlessly and apathetically with a frustrating sense that our lives lack any substantial center. It is much easier to *feel* than to *think*, but we may not always be able to avoid the responsibility for our unconsidered actions. The popularity of Salinger's work, however, suggests that many young people today prefer "feeling" to "thinking."

This school of thought to which Salinger (and many other writers for the *New Yorker*) appears to belong stems not from the wise and witty Sir James Barrie, but from a fictional character whom William Wiegand identifies with Salinger and Salinger himself mentions in "A Girl I Knew"—Goethe's young Werther. Like Salinger's Seymour, Werther shoots himself. Before his demise, however, he says, "Children are nearer to my heart than anything else on earth," and argues that we should treat them, "as God treats us—He makes us happiest when He lets us wander under the intoxication of agreeable illusions."

"The intoxication of agreeable illusions" describes very well the reasons some adults long nostalgically for childhood and are thus reluctant to discipline children intelligently. It also describes the pleasure received from the kind of *kitsch* which many people prefer to serious art. Such intoxication is, however, incompatible with mature achievement; and as long as Salinger remains under its influence—as he is when he writes about Seymour Glass—his art is likely to deteriorate. There is more than mere "envy" in Norman Mailer's observation that Salinger is "the greatest mind ever to stay in prep school."[9]

A Dora Copperfield Kind of Complex

We cannot criticize an artist, however, for working on his own terms. If Salinger wishes to devote himself to the search for the seer, that is his business. We can, however, feel some justifiable trepidation about the future of American literature if Salinger is considered—as he was, for example, in the recent *Saturday Review* poll—the most important artist the disappointing post-World War II period has produced. Since—despite the schemes of authoritarian regimes—we cannot manufacture significant artists to order, we must take what art we can get. Perhaps the general despair and moral paralysis caused by the overhanging shadow of nuclear destruction have made impossible in our age the development of dynamic, mature novelists who might offer us a more constructive vision than the wistful contemplation of the lost irresponsibility of childhood.

I do not believe, however, that we are in such a plight. Although I feel that writers like Norman Mailer and Jack Kerouac (who some faulty prophets once thought might supplant Salinger in youth's affection) have capitulated—in different ways—to the stresses of our time as much as Salinger, I find great encouragement in the tremendously witty but caustically critical short stories, novels, and plays of James Purdy. *Malcolm* and *The Nephew* avoid both the pique of the Beats and Salinger's wistful resignation, and they voice instead a mature anger that matches the appalling apathy of our times. Purdy's reputation is likely to grow more slowly than Salinger's, for he makes fewer concessions to the reader's sensibilities while making as stringent demands upon his attention. Purdy distresses readers, too, by suggesting—as Marc Rosenberg's comparison of *Malcolm* with *Catcher* points out—that we are really not "too sensitive" to cope with the "phony" world, but "too innocent" (in the sense of ignorant). Americans like to be considered sensitive, but they dislike being supposed innocent, despite the fact that in general they are actually much more innocent than sensitive. Purdy thus demands a strong-minded reader who has outgrown childish illusions about himself, and—like Walt Whitman—he challenges the time to produce such readers. Purdy proves, however, that we can still look for writers who have the quality Salinger lacks—an intellectual vision which makes them believe that life could still be an adventure if individuals would accept the challenge of their responsibilities. We need not yet be resigned to our time's remaining "The Age of Holden Caulfield."

As for the reclusive Salinger himself, he may—like William Faulkner, who after years of avoiding the public became surprisingly garrulous before his death—emerge from his hideout as his own children grow up. Faulkner is not a good parallel, though, for while he shunned critics, he was accessible to Hollywood. Salinger may follow the lead of writers like Emily Dickinson and Robinson Jeffers, who all their lives remained isolated from a society that affronted them.

While we wait to see whether Salinger or new writings emerge from his lair, we may be sure that for some time to come new readers by the hundreds of thousands will go on buying and reading his four published books. They get their money's worth. I cannot agree with those who minimize *Catcher*. It is probably the great portrait of the sensitive middle-class adolescent of our era which provides youth with plenty of everything except love and an acceptable sense of direction. Some of the short stories are even more effective dramatizations of the plight of those whom this age threatens to overwhelm. It is difficult to think of another half a dozen stories about the peculiar malaise of our "respectable" society, which has not really learned how to respect itself, that compare with "A Perfect Day for Bananafish," "Uncle Wiggily in Connecticut," "Down at the Dinghy," "For Esmé—with Love and Squalor," "Pretty Mouth and Green My Eyes," and "Franny."

"Elaine," "The Varioni Brothers," "The Last Day of the Last Furlough," and "I'm Crazy" also deserve to be brought out of their hiding places in old magazines, as remarkable evocations of the responses of frightened, sensitive people to serious predicaments engendered by their societies. Although "The Inverted Forest" and "De Daumier-Smith's Blue Period" are structurally unimpressive as works of art, they offer valuable insights into Salinger's concept of the artist. "Zooey," "Raise High the Roofbeam, Carpenters," and "Seymour: An Introduction" are, of course, despite their prolixity and sentimentality, indispensable embodiments of Salinger's vision of a "nice" world. But then Salinger—except during the early years of the war when he was seeking an audience—has really scarcely published anything that can simply be ignored by those seeking an understanding of his art and his personality. Although he advocates undiscriminating love, Salinger has been most discriminating about allowing the public to see what he produces.

Notes and References

Chapter One

1. Ernest Havemann, "The Search for the Mysterious J. D. Salinger," *Life*, November 3, 1961, p. 138.
2. [Jack Skow], "'Sonny,'" in Henry Anatole Grunwald, ed., *Salinger: A Critical and Personal Portrait* (New York, 1962), p 10. Hereafter material appearing in this book will be identified simply by the notation, Grunwald, *Salinger*.
3. *Ibid.*, p. 11.
4. *Ibid.*
5. Frederick Pillsbury, "Mysterious J. D. Salinger: The Untold Chapter of the Famous Writer's Years as a Valley Forge Cadet," Philadelphia *Sunday Bulletin Magazine*, October 29, 1961, pp. 23-24. All details about Salinger's career at Valley Forge derive from this article.
6. Havemann, *loc. cit.*
7. This awkward and sentimental lyric, which some of Salinger's friends deny he wrote, appears in the Pillsbury article and in Grunwald, *Salinger*, p. 12.
8. Grunwald, *Salinger*, p. 13, says that Salinger's father accompanied him, but William Maxwell—the closest adult acquaintance of Salinger's to write a biographical sketch about him—says that Salinger's father sent him abroad to write ads for an importing firm (*Book-of-the-Month Club News*, Midsummer, 1951, p. 6).
9. "Twin State Telescope," Claremont (New Hampshire) *Daily Eagle*, November 13, 1953.
10. Havemann, *loc. cit.*
11. See Whit Burnett's anthology *Firsts of the Famous* (New York, 1962), a collection from *Story* of the first published short stories of Nelson Algren, John Cheever, Truman Capote, Norman Mailer, Carson McCullers, Tennessee Williams, William Saroyan, and others. Salinger's "The Young Folks" is not included.
12. New York *Herald-Tribune Book Review*, August 19, 1951, p. 2.
13. Pillsbury, *loc. cit.*
14. *Ibid.*, p. 23.
15. William Maxwell, "J. D. Salinger," *Book-of-the-Month Club News*, Midsummer, 1951, p. 6.
16. Tom Davis, "J. D. Salinger: A Checklist," *Papers of the Bibliographical Society of America*, LIII, 69 (First Quarter, 1959).

17. "Contributors," *Story*, XXV, 1 (November-December, 1944).
18. Maxwell, *loc. cit.*
19. Havemann, *op. cit.*, p. 132.
20. *Ibid.*
21. Maxwell, *loc. cit.*
22. Richard Gehman, Introduction to *Best from Cosmopolitan* (Avon, 1961) discusses Salinger's vulgar response to Gehman's request to include "The Inverted Forest" in the collection. The novelette was included in the Diamond Jubilee Issue of *Cosmopolitan* (March, 1961), although Grunwald reports (*Salinger*, p. 20) that Salinger himself came out of seclusion to plead with one of the editors not to reprint it.
23. According to Jack Skow (Grunwald, *Salinger*, p. 14), Salinger often dated girls from the Barbizon Hotel for Women and gave them reading lists on Zen.
24. *Best American Short Stories of 1949* (Boston, 1949), p. 319.
25. "Backstage with Esquire," *Esquire*, October, 1945, p. 34. Salinger also told Herschel Brickell that he was "essentially a short-story writer" and that he would drop the project of writing a novel "if he feels he is abusing what talent he has, or spreading it too thin." (*Prize Stories of 1949* [New York, 1949], p. 249.)
26. Maxwell, *loc. cit.*
27. *Ibid.*
28. Charles Lee, *The Hidden Public* (Garden City, New York, 1958), p. 184.
29. William Poster, "Tomorrow's Child," *Commentary*, XIII, 90-92 (January, 1952).
30. Eloise Perry Hazard, "Eight Fictional Finds," *Saturday Review*, XXXV, 17 (February 16, 1952).
31. Pillsbury, *loc. cit.*
32. Gutwillig, Robert, "Everybody's Caught 'The Catcher in the Rye,'" *New York Times Book Review* (Paperback Section), January 15, 1961, p. 38.
33. "The Careful Young Men: Tomorrow's Leaders Analyzed by Today's Teachers," *Nation*, CLXXXIV, 200 (March 9, 1957). Kunitz' remarks were one of a group of contributions to a forum discussing leading influences on the present college generation. In the same colloquium, Carlos Baker mentions Salinger as the closest present competitor to Thomas Wolfe (p. 199).
34. Havemann, *op. cit.*, p. 135.
35. *Ibid.*, p. 137.
36. Donald Fiene has allowed me to examine a photostatic copy of the certificate of marriage, on which Salinger asserts that this is his first marriage.
37. *The Village Voice* (New York, March 8, 1962), p. 5.

Notes and References

38. Harrison Salisbury in the *New York Times*, February 9, 1962, p. 4.
39. "Modern American Classics," *Saturday Review*, XLV, 20 (February 17, 1962).
40. Frederick L. Gwynn and Joseph L. Blotner, eds., *Faulkner in the University* (Charlottesville, Virginia, 1959), p. 244. Faulkner goes on to say that Holden's story was about "an intelligent, very sensitive young man who—in this day and time was an anachronism, was almost an obsolescence, trying to cope with a struggle with the present-day world which he was not fitted for . . ." (p. 246).
41. *Publishers' Weekly*, CLXXX, 36 (September 18, 1961). The struggle was unavailing. I bought a copy of *Franny and Zooey*, for example, from a department store two weeks before the official publication date, at 38 per cent off the list price.
42. Lewis Nichols, "In and Out of Books," *New York Times Book Review*, November 19, 1961, p. 8.
43. Richard Bury, "Salinger," *Books and Bookmen* (London), VII, 8 (June, 1962).
44. William Faulkner, "On Privacy: The American Dream—What Happened to It?," *Harper's Magazine*, CCXI, 34 (July, 1955).
45. "Mysterious J. D. Salinger," *Newsweek*, May 30, 1960, p. 92.
46. Reviewed by Richard Sharp in *The Village Voice*, June 14, 1962, p. 9. Sharp found the production "pleases only to the extent that one recalls the book."
47. Maxwell, *loc. cit.*
48. J. D. Salinger, *Franny and Zooey* (Boston, 1961), p. 49.
49. J. D. Salinger, *The Catcher in the Rye* (Boston, 1951), p. 182.
50. J. D. Salinger, *"Raise High the Roof Beam, Carpenters"* and *"Seymour: An Introduction"* (Boston, [1963]), p. 114.
51. The Rev. Mr. Richard Hanson announced a sermon on "Franny and Zooey" on Sunday, October 22, 1961, at 11 A.M. (*The Village Voice*, October 19, 1961, p. 3.)

Chapter Two

1. Ihab Hassan, *Radical Innocence: Studies in the Contemporary American Novel* (Princeton, New Jersey, 1961), p. 263. (Also in Grunwald, *Salinger*, pp. 140-41.)
2. Grunwald, *Salinger*, p. xxvii, maintains that in Salinger's writing "phony" has "no exact contrary," but he is wrong. Holden Caulfield uses the word "nice" to describe what he likes just as he uses "phony" to describe what he dislikes. Perhaps the most significant occurrence of the word is in Holden's statement near the end of *The Catcher in the Rye* that the sight of Phoebe going around and around on the carousel makes him happy just because she

looks "so damn *nice*." Salinger favors the adjective himself. Discussing the reception of *Catcher* with Eloise Perry Hazard, he commented that "many of the letters from readers have been very nice." (*Saturday Review*, February 16, 1952, p. 17.)

3. J. D. Salinger, "Uncle Wiggily in Connecticut," *Nine Stories* (New York: Signet Books, 1954), p. 28.

4. This untitled poem in *War is Kind and Other Lines* begins "A man said to the Universe."

5. J. D. Salinger, *The Catcher in the Rye* (Boston, 1951), pp. 130-31.

6. David Riesman, *The Lonely Crowd* (Garden City, New York: Anchor Books, 1953), pp. 278, 277.

7. "Current Cinema," *New Yorker*, XXV, 75 (January 28, 1950).

8. *Motion Picture Herald*, October 22, 1949. I have not been able to examine a script of this film nor to view it. The reviews I have examined agree with this summary based upon a distributor's preview of the film. The quality of the film is not relevant to the comparison I wish to make between it and the short story.

Chapter Four

1. *Village Voice*, March 8, 1962, p. 6.

2. J. D. Salinger, *The Catcher in the Rye* (Boston, 1951), pp. 182-83.

3. F. Scott Fitzgerald, *The Great Gatsby*, Student's Edition (New York, n. d.), p. 154.

4. Gwynn and Blotner (*The Fiction of J. D. Salinger*, p. 17) wrongly equate the Kenneth Caulfield mentioned in this story with Holden. We learn in "The Last Day of the Last Furlough" that Vincent had not had a good time for four years before the beginning of this story—in which Holden is first reported as "missing in action." In "The Stranger," we learn that Vincent's girl friend had broken with him before he entered the service. Kenneth, therefore, could not possibly be the same character as Holden in this group of related stories. Kenneth is instead a prototype of Holden's younger brother Allie in *The Catcher in the Rye*. Allie's death is described in the novel as having the same effect upon Holden that Kenneth's is reported to have had upon Vincent in "The Stranger."

5. "Twin State Telescope," Claremont (New Hampshire) *Daily Eagle*, November 13, 1953.

Chapter Five

1. J. D. Salinger, "The Inverted Forest," *Cosmopolitan*, CL, 124 (March, 1961).

2. *Ibid.*, p. 132.

3. Ihab Hassan, *Radical Innocence*, p. 267.
4. Paul Levine, "J. D. Salinger: The Development of the Misfit Hero," *Twentieth Century Literature*, IV, 93-94 (October, 1958).
5. Gwynn and Blotner, *The Fiction of J. D. Salinger*, p. 14.
6. "The Inverted Forest," *op. cit.*, p. 119.

Chapter Six

1. In his interview with Shirley Blaney (Claremont, New Hampshire, *Daily Eagle*, November 13, 1953), Salinger said that he had worked before the war on the Swedish liner *M. S. Kungsholm*, which is mentioned in this story as one of the ships anchored in Havana harbor.
2. Why is Seymour fascinated by trees? "That funny business with the trees" that Muriel's mother mentions is never explained in the story; nor does it need to be for Seymour's condition to be understood. Gywnn and Blotner see this obsession as one of many suggestions that Seymour's "sexual inadequacy" is an underlying motif of the story. While Seymour's childish behavior certainly suggests that he may crave other forms of attention to compensate for a real or imagined lack of virility, I believe an explanation of his propensity for trees that is more in keeping with his enthusiasm for Rilke may be found in those lines of the *First Duino Elegy* translated by J. B. Leishman and Stephen Spender:

> . . . already the knowing brutes are aware
> that we don't feel very securely at home
> within our interpreted world. There remains, perhaps,
> some tree on a slope, to be looked at day after day. . . .

Seymour is surely not "very securely at home" in the world. Although he probably drove into trees to attract attention, he may also have felt the kind of response to them that Rilke describes in this passage. Perhaps he even felt an irrational urge to disrupt violently their firmly rooted composure. Undoubtedly the infatuation also reflects a longing to merge oneself with simple, uncomplicated nature.
3. Grunwald, *Salinger*, p. 127.

Chapter Seven

1. Gwynn and Blotner, *The Fiction of J. D. Salinger*, p. 14.
2. Three years later Salinger uses this same image of the paper flapping against a lamppost in an interview to describe the way in which he expects someday to see the embarrassing photograph on the dust-jacket of *The Catcher in the Rye* similarly discarded. (Eloise Perry Hazard, "Eight Fictional Finds," *Saturday Review*, XXXV, 17

[February 6, 1952].) Obviously it was deeply rooted in his mind. The repetition of the image suggests that sudden acclaim frightened Salinger because he feared the heart-breaking disillusionment that might occur if he allowed his success to go to his head and then sank back into obscurity. He obviously had little confidence in the emotional stability of either himself or his admirers.

3. John Edward Hardy, *Commentaries on Five Modern American Short Stories* (Frankfurt am Main, Germany, 1962), pp. 7-10. The other stories are by Faulkner, Hemingway, Carson McCullers, and Truman Capote.

4. James Joyce, *Stephen Hero* (New York, 1955), p. 211. The fragmentary manuscript was first published in 1944. I do not claim that Joyce influenced Salinger—only that Salinger's stories illustrate Joyce's theories.

5. James Joyce, *A Portrait of the Artist as a Young Man* (New York: Compass Books, 1956), p. 204.

Chapter Eight

1. Warren French with Marc Rosenberg, "The Beast that Devours Its Young," *CCC: The Journal of the Conference on Composition and Communication*, XIII, 7 (May, 1962).

2. Ernest Havemann, "The Search for the Mysterious J. D. Salinger," *Life* (November 3, 1961), p. 141.

3. Grunwald, *Salinger*, p. 255.

4. *Ibid.*, p. 151.

5. *Ibid.*, p. 252.

6. J. D. Salinger, *"Raise High the Roof Beam, Carpenters"* and *"Seymour: An Introduction"* (Boston, [1963]), p. 123.

7. R. G. G. Price, "Booking Office," *Punch*, CCXXI, 192 (August 15, 1951).

8. Grunwald, *Salinger*, pp. 125-26.

9. Hugh MacLean, "Conservatism in Modern American Fiction," *College English*, XV, 317 (March, 1954).

10. David Leitch, "The Salinger Myth," *Twentieth Century*, No. 168 (November, 1960), p. 431. Grunwald does not reproduce the footnote containing this figure.

11. Price, *loc. cit.*

12. This imaginative and allusive Norwegian title has led to a fascinating correspondence. The translation given has been graciously supplied by Rolf L. Bergendahl, Cultural Attaché of the Norwegian Embassy in Washington, who explains that the literal translation is "Each Takes His—And the Rest of Us Gets None," which would not convey the proverbial connotations of the Norwegian title. Gerard

Notes and References

Vanneck of the United Nations Terminology Unit, New York, further explains that the title is derived from the words of a familiar Norwegian children's singing game and that the general idea of the title might best be conveyed by "Odd Man Out." Donald Fiene informs me that translator Åke Fen, shortly before his death, received an annual Norwegian Translators' Society award for his rendition of *The Catcher in the Rye*.

13. Quoted in W. S. Field, "Hermann Hesse as Critic of English and American Literature," *Monatshefte*, LIII, 156 (April-May, 1961).

14. The bibliography in *American Literature* for May, 1962, lists an article, "J. D. Salinger" in Japanese by Hisao Kanesaki in *Jimbun Kenkyu*, a publication of the University of Osaka, for June, 1961. Donald Fiene is preparing a bibliography of other foreign reactions to Salinger. One of the most interesting foreign criticisms of *The Catcher in the Rye* is Panova's "J. D. Salinger's Novel," *Inostrannaya Literatura* (Foreign Literature), November, 1960, pp. 138-41, prepared to accompany a translation of the novel which appeared in that issue of the magazine. Miss Panova denounces Holden as a *stilyaga* (Russian Beatnik) with many unacceptable traits, yet finds him ultimately sympathetic because he is a victim of a heartless capitalistic society symbolized by the sated funeral director Ossenburger, who "grows rich on the mortality of the poor."

15. Since this chapter was written, the German translation of *The Catcher in the Rye* has been "reworked" by the distinguished German novelist, Heinrich Böll, author of *Billiards at Half Past Nine*, and published with the title literally translated *Der Fänger im Roggen*. The employment of an artist of such stature to revise the translation suggests the increasing importance that is being attached to Salinger's novel in Europe.

16. *New York Times Book Review*, January 7, 1962, p. 8.

Chapter Nine

1. J. D. Salinger, *"Raise High the Roof Beam, Carpenters" and "Seymour: An Introduction"* (Boston, [1963]), p. 205.

2. For some reason, it turns out that Zooey Glass was in 1942 in the hands of what sounds like the same examining group (J. D. Salinger, *Franny and Zooey*, p. 55). Since Zooey, like Teddy, has a sister several years younger than himself, the reader is left to figure out for himself whether Salinger just liked the kind of characters that attract such examining boards or whether Zooey is a considerably more charming reincarnation of Teddy. Perhaps "Teddy" can be fitted into the Glass legend.

3. Grunwald, *Salinger*, p. 184.

4. *Ibid.*, p. 153.
5. William Maxwell, "J. D. Salinger," *Book-of-the-Month-Club News*, Midsummer, 1951, p. 6.

Chapter Ten

1. *The Village Voice*, March 8, 1962, p. 6.
2. Grunwald, *Salinger*, pp. 55-56.
3. Burling Lowrey, "Salinger and the House of Glass," *New Republic*, CXLI, 23 (October 26, 1959).
4. Some may wonder about the relationship between Holden and a boy named Curtis Caulfield, who makes a brief appearance in "Seymour" (page 225 in the book version). My guess is that there is none. Curtis does seem just the kind of red herring that Salinger would employ to tease those who insisted upon working out too literal interrelations between all details in his fiction.
5. "Mysterious J. D. Salinger," *Newsweek*, May 30, 1960, p. 92.

Chapter Eleven

1. Donald M. Fiene, "From a Study of Salinger: Controversy in the Catcher," *The Realist*, No. 30, pp. 1, 23-25 (December, 1961-January, 1962). Fiene reports that the book has proved especially objectionable—as might be anticipated—in South Africa. Mrs. Levin describes her experiences in "J. D. Salinger in Oklahoma," *Chicago Jewish Forum*, XIX, 231-33 (Spring, 1961).
2. Edward P. J. Corbett, "Raise High the Barriers, Censors," *America*, CIV, 441-43 (January 7, 1961).
3. Hugh MacLean, "Conservatism in Modern American Fiction," *College English*, XV, 317 (March, 1954).
4. Wayne C. Booth, *The Rhetoric of Fiction* (Chicago, 1961), p. 287.
5. Kingsley Widmer, "The American Road," *University of Kansas City Review*, XXVI, 314 (June, 1960).
6. Warren French with Marc Rosenberg, "The Beast That Devours Its Young," *CCC: The Journal of the Conference on College Composition and Communication*, XIII, 7 (May, 1962). The article contrasts *Catcher* with James Purdy's *Malcolm*.
7. Paul Goodman, *Growing Up Absurd* (New York, 1960), p. 12.
8. David Riesman, *The Lonely Crowd* (Garden City, New York: Anchor Books, 1953), p. 278.
9. Norman Mailer, *Advertisements for Myself* (New York, 1959), p. 467.

Selected Bibliography

PRIMARY SOURCES

1. *Books*

The Catcher in the Rye. Boston: Little, Brown and Company, 1951. Reprint editions: New York: Grosset and Dunlap, 1952; New York: New American Library (paperback), 1953; New York: Modern Library, 1958; New York: Bantam Books (paperback), 1964.

Franny and Zooey. Boston: Little, Brown and Company, 1961. Reprint edition: New York: Bantam Books (paperback), 1964.

Nine Stories ["A Perfect Day for Bananafish," "Uncle Wiggily in Connecticut," "Just Before the War with the Eskimos," "The Laughing Man," "Down at the Dinghy," "For Esmé—With Love and Squalor," "Pretty Mouth and Green My Eyes,' "De Daumier-Smith's Blue Period," "Teddy"]. Boston: Little, Brown and Company, 1953. Reprint editions: New York: New American Library (paperback), 1954; New York: Modern Library, 1959; New York: Bantam Books (paperback), 1964.

"Raise High the Roof Beam, Carpenters" and "Seymour: An Introduction." Boston: Little, Brown and Company, 1963. Reprint edition: New York: Bantam Books (paperback), 1965.

Note: An unauthorized paperback, *The Complete Uncollected Short Stories of J. D. Salinger*, Volumes 1 and 2, apparently published by an unidentified source in Berkeley, California, is reported in the *New York Times*, November 3, 1974, p. 1. Exact contents not listed. The book has been suppressed by the copyright holders as a piracy.

2. *Short Stories*

"Blue Melody," *Cosmopolitan*, CXXV (September, 1948), 50–51, 112–19.

"Both Parties Concerned," *Saturday Evening Post*, CCXVI (February 20, 1944), 14, 47–48.

"A Boy in France," *Saturday Evening Post*, CCXVII (March 31, 1945), 21, 92. Reprinted in *Post Stories, 1942–1945*, ed. by Ben Hibbs (New York: Random House, 1946), pp. 314–20.

"De Daumier-Smith's Blue Period," *World Review* (London), N.S., no. 39 (May, 1952), 33–48. Reprinted in *Nine Stories*.

"Down at the Dinghy," *Harper's*, CXCVIII (April, 1949), 87–91. Reprinted in *Nine Stories*.

"Elaine," *Story*, XXVI (March–April, 1945), 38–47.

"For Esmé–With Love and Squalor," *New Yorker*, XXVI (April 8, 1950), 28–36. Reprinted in *World Review* (London), N.S., no. 18 (August, 1950), 44–59; in *Prize Stories of 1950: The O. Henry Awards*, ed. by Herschel Brickell (Garden City, N. Y.: Doubleday & Co., 1950), pp. 244–64; in *Fifty Great Short Stories*, ed. by Milton Crane (New York: Bantam Books, 1952), pp. 252–75; in *Nine Stories*; and in several college textbooks.

"Franny," *New Yorker*, XXX (January 29, 1955), 23–43. Reprinted in *Franny and Zooey*.

"A Girl I Knew," *Good Housekeeping*, CXXVI (February, 1948), 37, 186–96. Reprinted in *Best American Short Stories of 1949*, ed. by Martha J. Foley (Boston: Houghton Mifflin Co., 1949), pp. 248–60.

"Go See Eddie," *University of Kansas City Review*, VII (December, 1940), 121–24. [Described in Warren French, "An Unnoticed Salinger Story," *College English*, XXVI (1965), 294–95.]

"The Hang of It," *Collier's*, CVIII (July 12, 1941), 22.

"Hapworth 16, 1924," *New Yorker*, XLI (June 19, 1965), 32–113.

"The Heart of a Broken Story," *Esquire*, XVI (September, 1941), 32, 131–33.

"I'm Crazy," *Collier's*, CXVI (December 22, 1945), 36, 48, 51.

"The Inverted Forest," *Cosmopolitan*, CXXIII (December, 1947), 73–109; reprinted, CL (Diamond Jubilee Issue, March, 1961), 111–32.

"Just Before the War with the Eskimos," *New Yorker*, XXIV (June 5, 1948), 37–46. Reprinted in *Prize Stories of 1949*, ed. by Herschel Brickell (Garden City, N.Y.: Doubleday & Co., 1949), pp. 249–61; in *Nine Stories*; and in *Manhattan: Stories from the Heart of a Great City*, ed. by Seymour Krim (New York: Bantam Books, 1954), pp. 22–35.

"Last Day of the Last Furlough," *Saturday Evening Post*, CCXVII (July 15, 1944), 26–27, 61–64.

"The Laughing Man," *New Yorker*, XXV (March 19, 1949), 27–32; reprinted in *Nine Stories*.

"The Long Debut of Lois Taggett," *Story*, XXI (September–October, 1942), 28–34. Reprinted in *Story: The Fiction of the Forties*, ed. by Whit and Hallie S. Burnett (New York: Dutton, 1949), pp. 153–62.

"Once a Week Won't Kill You," *Story*, XXV (November–December, 1944), 23–27.

Selected Bibliography

"A Perfect Day for Bananafish," *New Yorker*, XXIII (January 31, 1948), 21–25. Reprinted in *55 Short Stories from the New Yorker* (New York: Simon and Schuster, 1949), pp. 144–55; and in *Nine Stories*.

"Personal Notes of an Infantryman," *Collier's*, CX (December 12, 1942), 96.

"Pretty Mouth and Green My Eyes," *New Yorker*, XXVII (July 14, 1951), 20–24. Reprinted in *Nine Stories*; also in *Anthology of Famous American Short Stories*, ed. by J. A. Burrell and B. A. Cerf (New York: Modern Library, 1953), pp. 1297–1306.

"Raise High the Roof Beam, Carpenters," *New Yorker*, XXXI (November 19, 1955), 51–116. Reprinted in *Short Stories from the New Yorker, 1950–1960* (New York: Simon and Schuster, 1960), pp. 49–65, and in book form with "Seymour: An Introduction."

"Seymour: An Introduction," *New Yorker*, XXXV (June 6, 1959), 42–111. Reprinted in book form with "Raise High the Roof Beam, Carpenters."

"Slight Rebellion Off Madison," *New Yorker*, XXII (December 21, 1946), 76–79.

"Soft-Boiled Sergeant," *Saturday Evening Post*, CCXVI (April 15, 1944), 18, 82–85.

"The Stranger," *Collier's*, CXVI (December 1, 1945), 18, 77.

"Teddy," *New Yorker*, XXVIII (January 31, 1953), 26–38. Reprinted in *Nine Stories*.

"This Sandwich Has No Mayonnaise," *Esquire*, XXV (October, 1945), 54–56, 147–49. Reprinted in *The Armchair Esquire*, ed. by Arnold Gingrich and L. Rust Hills (New York: Putnam's, 1958), pp. 187–97.

"Uncle Wiggily in Connecticut," *New Yorker*, XXIV (March 20, 1948), 30–36. Reprinted in *Nine Stories*; also in *Short Story Masterpieces*, ed. by Robert Penn Warren and Albert Erskine (New York: Dell, 1954), pp. 408–23.

"The Varioni Brothers," *Saturday Evening Post*, CCXVI (July 17, 1943), 12–13, 76–77.

"The Young Folks," *Story*, XVI (March–April, 1940), 26–30.

"A Young Girl in 1941 with No Waist at All," *Mademoiselle*, XXV (May, 1947), 222–23, 292–302.

"Zooey," *New Yorker*, XXXIII (May 4, 1957), 32–139. Reprinted in *Franny and Zooey*.

SECONDARY SOURCES

1. Biography

FOSBURGH, LACEY. "J. D. Salinger Speaks about His Silence," *New York Times*, November 3, 1974, pp. 1, 69. Report of a unique telephone interview in which Salinger announced he was still writing, but denounced the unauthorized publication of his uncollected stories as "a terrible invasion of my privacy."

HAVEMANN, ERNEST. "The Search for the Mysterious J. D. Salinger," *Life*, LI (November 3, 1961), 129–44. Report of an unsuccessful effort to interview Salinger at his Cornish, New Hampshire, retreat; illustrated with photographs made with a telephoto lens.

MAXWELL, WILLIAM. "J. D. Salinger," *Book-of-the-Month Club News*, Midsummer, 1951, pp. 5–6. Fullest, most sympathetic account of Salinger's life up to the publication of *The Catcher in the Rye* by a fellow novelist on the *New Yorker* editorial staff.

PILLSBURY, FREDERICK. "Mysterious J. D. Salinger: The Untold Chapter of the Famous Writer's Years as a Valley Forge Cadet," Philadelphia *Sunday Bulletin Magazine*, October 29, 1961, pp. 23–24. Invaluable account of Salinger's cadet days drawn from official records of the Valley Forge Military Academy.

[SKOW, JACK]. "Sonny: An Introduction," *Time*, LXVIII (September 15, 1961), 84–90. Most detailed account of Salinger's life compiled from materials assembled by *Time*'s research staff.

2. *Bibliography*

BEEBE, MAURICE and JENNIFER SPERRY. "Criticism of J. D. Salinger: A Selected Checklist." *Modern Fiction Studies*, XII (Autumn, 1966), 377–90. Lists only criticisms in English and includes a valuable story-by-story breakdown of relevant passages.

FIENE, DONALD M. "J. D. Salinger: A Bibliography," *Wisconsin Studies in Contemporary Literature*, IV (Winter, 1963), 109–49. Extensive listing of Salinger's publications, foreign translations of them, and reviews and criticisms of his works published in many languages throughout the world.

3. *Collections of Criticism*

BELCHER, WILLIAM F. and JAMES W. LEE, eds. *J. D. Salinger and the Critics*. Belmont, Cal.: Wadsworth, 1962. Contains John Skow's "Sonny: An Introduction"; ten general articles on Salinger; thirteen on *The Catcher in the Rye*.

GRUNWALD, HENRY ANATOLE, ed. *Salinger: A Critical and Personal Portrait*. New York: Harper and Brothers, 1962. Contains a long introduction by the editor; Skow's biography; some two dozen articles, mostly laudatory; many are reprinted and others written specifically for this first collection.

LASER, MARVIN and NORMAN FRUMAN, eds. *Studies in J. D. Salinger: Reviews, Essays and Critiques of "The Catcher in the Rye" and Other Fiction*. New York: Odyssey Press, 1963. Reprints thirty-four articles including four explications of "For Esmé—With Love and Squalor," along with editorial comments.

Selected Bibliography

MARSDEN, MALCOLM M., ed. *If You Really Want to Know: A "Catcher" Casebook.* Chicago and elsewhere: Scott, Foresman and Co., 1963. Least valuable of the "casebooks"; contains early reviews and thirteen complete articles on the novel but only excerpts from sixteen others.

Modern Fiction Studies, XII, 3 (Autumn, 1966). Contains, besides the Beebe-Sperry bibliography (see above), original articles by John Antico, Brother Fidelian Burke, F. S. C., Hubert I. Cohen, Bernice and Sanford Goldstein, John V. Hagopian, John M. Howell, and John Russell.

SIMONSON, HAROLD P. and PHILIP E. HAGER, eds. *Salinger's "Catcher in the Rye": Clamor vs. Criticism.* Boston: D. C. Heath and Co., 1963. Reprints twenty-two articles about the novel only, along with news reports about censorship attempts.

"Special Number: Salinger," *Wisconsin Studies in Contemporary Literature,* IV, 1 (Winter, 1963). Contains, besides Donald Fiene's bibliography (see above) and a slightly reworded version of Chapter Two of this book, original essays by Sam Baskett, Joseph Blotner, Tom Davis, Ihab Hassan, John Lyons, John Russell, Arthur Schwartz, and Carl F. Strauch.

4. Individual Critical Essays

Almost all worthwhile criticism of Salinger published before 1962 appears in one or more of the collections listed above. Only a few exceptions are listed below, along with more recent articles that do not simply repeat—like many—earlier arguments.

On Salinger's Entire Work

COLES, ROBERT. "Reconsideration: J. D. Salinger," *New Republic,* CLXVIII (April 28, 1973), 30–32. Landmark criticism that describes how early enthusiasts, temporarily alienated from Salinger during activist years, are returning to his work since "we so far have not shown ourselves able to absorb and use the wisdom he has offered us."

FRENCH, WARREN. "The Age of Salinger." In *The Fifties: Fiction, Poetry, Drama,* pp. 1–39. Deland, Fla.: Everett/Edwards, 1971. Survey of the principal writings of the decade culminating in a long consideration of Salinger's writings as representative of a pervasive defeatism.

————. "Steinbeck and J. D. Salinger." In *Steinbeck's Literary Dimension,* ed. by Tetsumaro Hayashi, pp. 105–15. Metuchen, N.J.: Scarecrow Press, 1973. Compares the two writers as providing "one of those perennially essential refurbishings of the American literary idiom."

GILES, BARBARA. "The Lonely War of J. D. Salinger," *Mainstream*, XII (February, 1959), 2–13. The only important uncollected article from 1950s exemplifies the radical "party line" by taking Salinger to task for avoiding discussion of real social problems.

GOLDSTEIN, BERNICE and SANFORD. "Some Zen References in Salinger," *Literature East and West*, XV (1971), 83–95.

————. "Zen and Salinger," *Modern Fiction Studies*, XII (Autumn, 1966), 313–24. Elementary introductions to the principles of Zen philosophy pointing out its influences on Salinger.

GWYNN, FREDERICK L. and JOSEPH L. BLOTNER. *The Fiction of J. D. Salinger*. Pittsburgh: University of Pittsburgh Press, 1958. Although many interpretations of individual stories in this earliest monograph about Salinger have since been challenged, it provides a detailed summary of early response to his work.

HAMILTON, KENNETH. *J. D. Salinger: A Critical Essay*. Grand Rapids, Mich.: Eerdmans, 1967. Part of a series of pamphlets on "Contemporary Writers in Christian Perspective," this sensitive reading incorporates material from Hamilton's articles about the relationship of Salinger's work to Christian and other religious traditions.

MILLER, JAMES E., JR. *J. D. Salinger*. University of Minnesota Pamphlets on American Writers No. 51. Minneapolis: University of Minnesota Press, 1965. Outstanding short account of Salinger's career by a distinguished humanist who finds "alienation" the dominant theme in the fiction and concludes that Salinger deserves "a place in the first rank, and even, perhaps the preeminent position" in post–World War II American fiction.

SCHULZ, MAX F. "J. D. Salinger and the Crisis of Consciousness." In *Radical Sophistication: Studies in Contemporary Jewish-American Novelists*, pp. 198–217. Athens: Ohio University Press, 1969. Describes Buddy Glass's finding a way out of a cul-de-sac in attempting to present Seymour to readers by at last letting us see one of his brother's own writings in "Hapworth 16, 1924."

WEINBERG, HELEN. *The New Novel in America: The Kafkan Mode in Contemporary Fiction*. Ithaca, N.Y.: Cornell University Press, 1970. Beginning by attacking psychological criticism of Salinger, Weinberg presents his "emergent vision" as "one of the potential of the spiritual self."

WIEGAND, WILLIAM. "Salinger and Kierkegaard," *Minnesota Review*, V (May–July, 1965), 137–56. Presents carefully researched, scholarly case that Kierkegaard's philosophy illuminates both the form and the content of the Glass family saga.

On The Catcher in the Rye

BRYAN, JAMES. "The Psychological Structure of *The Catcher in the Rye*," *PMLA*, LXXXIX (October, 1974), 1065–74. Provides

Selected Bibliography

a psychoanalytical reading of the novel; sees in Holden's thoughts and actions a pattern of largely sexual aggression and withdrawal.

LEVINE, PAUL. "The Politics of Alienation," *Mosaic*, II, 1 (Fall, 1968), 3–17. Describes Holden's pilgrimage as "a pathetic rather than tragic" phenomenon of the Eisenhower years because the boy has no standard of reference other than society's and can find no sub-culture with which he can identify.

NOLAND, RICHARD W. "The Novel of Personal Formula: J. D. Salinger," *University Review*, XXXIII (Autumn, 1966), 19–24. Views this type of novel with displeasure as a quest for "the spontaneous, the natural, the instinctive, and the irrational"— an example of what Raymond Williams calls "the novel of personal formula."

TROWBRIDGE, CLINTON W. "The Symbolic Structure of *The Catcher in the Rye*," *Sewanee Review*, LXXIV (Summer, 1966), 681–693. Most detailed of several related analyses; Trowbridge explains Salinger's artistic techniques in presenting "the plight of the idealist in the modern world."

VANDERBILT, KERMIT. "Symbolic Resolution in *The Catcher in the Rye*: The Cap, the Carrousel, and the American West," *Western Humanities Review*, XVII (Summer, 1963), 271–77. Surprising regional essay points out that Holden goes West to recover his health and discover a new life.

On Nine Stories

BRYAN, JAMES E. "J. D. Salinger: The Fat Lady and the Chicken Sandwich," *College English*, XXIII (December, 1961), 226–29. Explication of the Christian symbolism in "Just Before the War with the Eskimos" which Bryan reads as a precursor to the story of the "Fat Lady" in "Zooey."

————. "A Reading of 'For Esmé—with Love and Squalor,' " *Criticism*, IX (Summer, 1967), 275–88. Sees Sergeant X as saved "not from, but *through* squalor to become a normal man equipped with the faculty to love for normal life."

————. "A Reading of Salinger's 'Teddy,' " *American Literature*, XL (November, 1968), 352–69. Points out the story's place in the structure of *Nine Stories* and the "coherent and terrible artistic vision" it offers even those who cannot accept mysticism.

GOLDSTEIN, BERNICE and SANFORD. "Zen and *Nine Stories*," *Renascence*, XXII (Summer, 1970), 171–82. Distinguishes between the characters who achieve *satori* and those who fail.

STEIN, WILLIAM BYSSHE. "Salinger's 'Teddy': *Tat Tvam Asi* or That Thou Art," *Arizona Quarterly*, XXIX (1973), 253–65. Describes how Teddy's encounters with others reveal their spiritual igno-

J. D. SALINGER

rance and contrast "the sterility of institutional Christianity with the vitality of traditional Vedantic thought."

On the Gospels of the Glass Family

DETWEILER, ROBERT. *Four Spiritual Crises in Mid-Century American Fiction.* Gainesville: University of Florida Monographs, Humanities No. 14; Fall, 1963. Pp. 36–43. Painstaking analysis of the religious aspects of Franny's breakdown and cure that leads to the conclusion that the stories do not ring true because of Salinger's "inability or unwillingness to see the existence and power of evil."

GLAZIER, LYLE. "The Glass Family Saga: Argument and Epiphany," *College English,* XXVII (December, 1965), 248–51. Points out that in both Glass family books, the first narrative is a poetic epiphany and the second, "a more prosaic argument for humanism."

RANLY, ERNEST W. "Journey to the East," *Commonweal,* XCVII (February 23, 1973), 465–69. Account of the writer's "coming home" to the East through Western writers—Ram Dass, Jesus, Hesse, and Salinger.

SEITZMAN, DANIEL. "Salinger's 'Franny': Homoerotic Imagery," *American Imago,* XXII (Spring–Summer, 1965), 57–76.

————. "Therapy and Antitherapy in Salinger's 'Zooey,'" *American Imago,* XXV (Summer, 1968), 140–62. Elaborate psychoanalytical interpretations that suffer from Seitzman's treating the characters as if they were real people rather than Salinger's fictional creations.

On "Hapworth 16, 1924"

GOLDSTEIN, BERNICE and SANFORD. "Ego and 'Hapworth 16, 1924,'" *Renascence,* XXIV (Spring, 1972), 159–67. Argues that Seymour's long letter is in Zen Style and illustrates his principal problem of continuing to deepen his own awareness while trying to break the barrier between the enlightened and the non-enlightened.

QUAGLIANO, ANTHONY. "'Hapworth 16, 1924': A Problem in Hagiography," *University of Dayton Review,* VIII, ii (Fall, 1971), 35–43. Portrays Salinger as writing the biography of Seymour as a contemporary American saint whose suicide is an attainment of the highest spirituality.

SLETHAUG, GORDON E. "Seymour: A Clarification," *Renascence,* XXIII (Spring, 1971), 115–28. Argues that Seymour must fulfill the dictates of God, so that his suicide has nothing to do with alienation from society or escapism.

See also JAMES E. MILLER, JR. *J. D. Salinger* (cited above), pp. 42–44.

Index

Index